Dedicated To My Parents

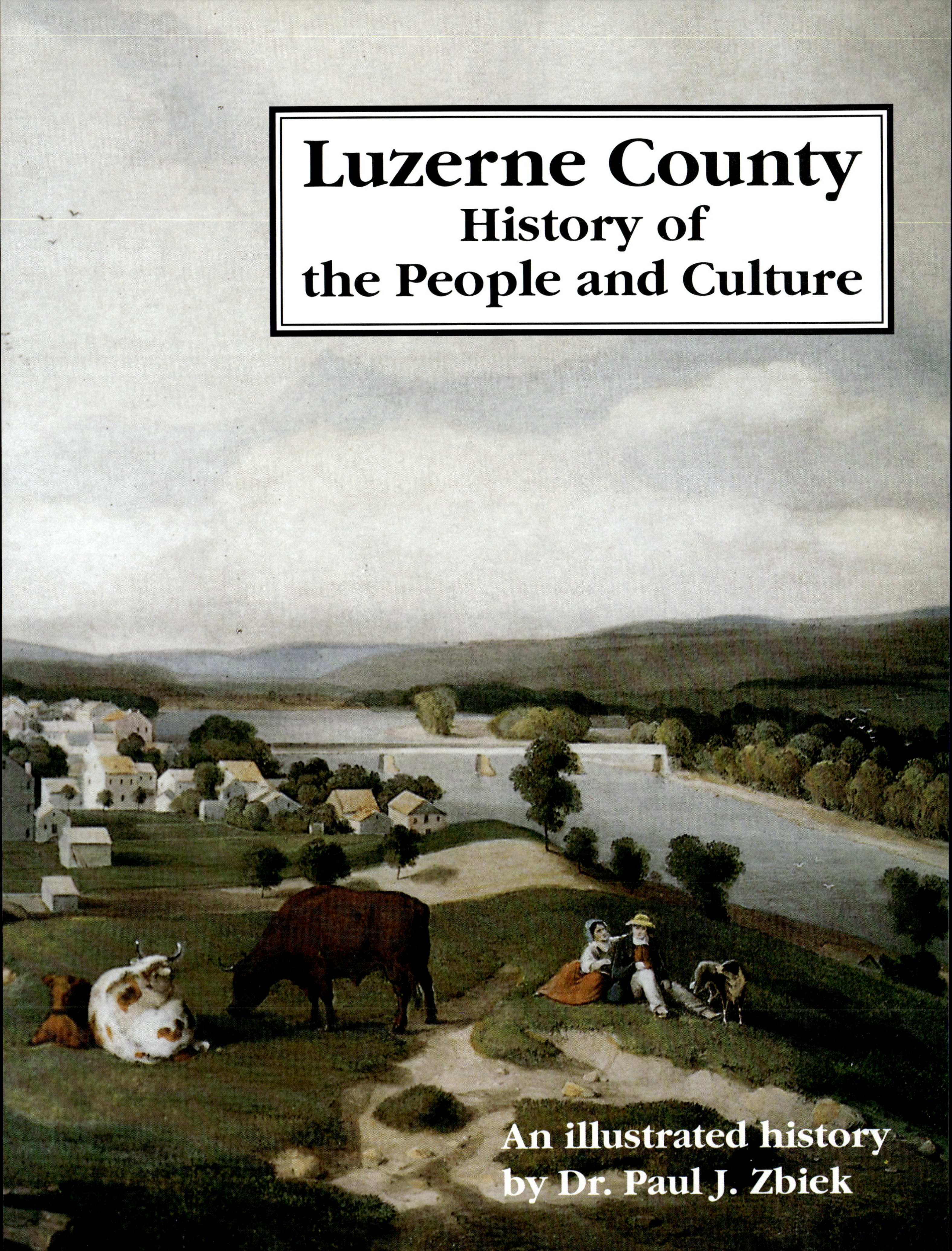

Luzerne County
History of the People and Culture

An illustrated history
by Dr. Paul J. Zbiek

LUZERNE COUNTY
History of the People and Culture

An Illustrated History
By Dr. Paul J. Zbiek

Edited by:
Sally Teller Lottick

Associate Editors:
Mary Ruth Kelly
F. Charles Petrillo
Clement Valletta

Photo Editor:
Michael Thomas

Staff:
Wyoming Historical and Geological Society

Mary Ruth Kelly	Executive Director
Barbara Ziemer	Business Manager
Cynthia Chapman	Librarian
Ruth Bevan	Library Assistant

Production:
Produced in cooperation with Bedwick and Jones, Inc.

Peg Jones	Vice President
Karen Fritzges	Layout and Design Consultant and Art Direction

---

Published in cooperation with Strategic Publications.
Printed in the United States of America.

Strategic Publications
140 Main Street Suite 208 | 322 Lancaster Avenue
Charlestown, MA 02129 | Lancaster, PA, 17603
Tracey L. Henk | President and Publisher

Library of Congress Cataloging in Publication Data
ISBN 0-937537-05-5

Zbiek, Dr. Paul J.
Luzerne County: History of the People and Culture
an illustrated history
Includes bibliography, photo credits and index.

*Previous page–
Early view of Wilkes-Barre from the Franklin Street Hill.*

Contents

INTRODUCTION

Land of Contrasts .10

CHAPTER ONE

People of the Woodlands and Frontier . . .20

CHAPTER TWO

Builders of a New Era 32

CHAPTER THREE

New Cultures and Old Traditions 50

CHAPTER FOUR

Anthracite and Agriculture 74

CHAPTER FIVE

Legacy of the Past, Hope for the Future . .90

CHAPTER SIX

Partners in Progress 108

Preface 6 • Bibliography 140 • Index 141

Preface

In *Luzerne County: History of the People and Culture* I have attempted to write a broad social history. This "people's history" seeks to demonstrate how the residents of the county have affected its development, along with the way such factors as geography and economics impacted upon the people. The recurring theme of the work is how the many different cultural, political, and economic forces achieved some sense of unity. While conflict between opposing factions was often the case, there was also a great deal of consensus building occurring simultaneously. This desire to find a common ground is a hallmark of both Luzerne County's past and present.

It is hoped that this work can be helpful at all levels of interest in local history. As with any broad history, it was often difficult to decide what to include. Although I tried for balance and objectivity, I am certain that omissions and biases have occurred. For these I apologize.

As with any historical work, the list of people who deserve credit goes far beyond the author. I would like to extend my deepest gratitude to all of the following contributors.

Michael Thomas' photographic editing and the high quality of his work are a major attribute of this book. His enthusiasm and the initiative he expended in locating images not previously published are especially valuable. Although there are illustrations that will be familiar to history buffs, there are a number of newly discovered treasures which will delight every reader.

Tracey Henk carried the project from its original inception through a major change in ownership to its current stage of completion. She has provided invaluable expertise in book publishing as well as a clear vision of the finished product. Mary Ruth Kelly, Executive Director of the Wyoming Historical and Geological Society, was responsible for coordinating efforts throughout the whole process. The Society's Publications Committee, Board and Staff provided crucial support for the project, and individual members made major financial and personal contributions. F.Charles Petrillo and Clement Valletta furnished editorial help, and both, along with Robert Janosov, assisted with historical advice.

Of all those associated with the Wyoming Historical and Geological Society, I would like to give special thanks to Sally Teller Lottick. Sally served as chief editor for this manuscript. Her suggestions, criticisms, patience, and time were invaluable. Sally's talents covered the full spectrum from basic writing style and grammar to a deep knowledge of our local history. Much of the quality of this book can be attributed to her commitment to solid editing and objective scholarship.

The support and assistance of Peg and Bob Jones of Bedwick and Jones, and the computer and layout skills of staff members Karen Fritzges and Janet Gow have been invaluable. A number of people at King's College rendered assistance through financial, professional, and personal support. I am grateful to Donald Farmer, Academic Vice President, and William Shergalis, Dean of the College of Arts and Sciences, along with my colleagues in the History Department,

A 19th century engraving of Nanticoke Dam (top) and Bear Creek and Bear Creek Boulevard (right).

Donald Stevens, Brian Pavlac, and Daniel Curran. Whether it was securing funding for my research or simply giving me good advice, they were always there when I needed them. I cannot forget the late Edward Hanlon. His earlier work on the history of Wyoming Valley was the inspiration behind this study.

My history students at King's College deserve my gratitude. Those in my Topics in Community History seminars, particularly Paula Raddick, deserve special recognition. Their ideas and research helped guide me throughout my study of Luzerne County. I also wish to thank Faculty Assistants Anita Grigor, Supervisor, Betty Didgeon, Donna Kazmierski, and Sandy Kase. Whether it was completing a rush typing job or helping me deal with an uncooperative computer, they always responded with the highest degree of professionalism combined with humor and patience.

The resources of the public libraries in the region, as well as those of the college and university libraries, have been essential to this work. Without these libraries' collections, no local history work would be possible.

My family deserves more appreciation than I can ever extend. My wife, Donna, served as a staunch supporter, an editorial critic, and a traveling companion in my desire to visit every community and roadway in Luzerne County. Her only comments regarding my hours spent in research and writing have been ones of support. Jason and Brandon, my stepsons, were always willing to give up the computer and give me encouragement. My parents, Edward and Ann Zbiek, have helped me through every step of my academic career. They also gave me an intense appreciation and understanding for my heritage and home—Luzerne County.

Finally, I thank the people who have lived, and now live, in Luzerne County. It is your story that I wish to tell and your lives I hope to honor.

Paul J. Zbiek

October 1994

Early views of Harvey's Lake (left) and Bear Creek c. 1910 (below).

A view of Reynolds' Woods, Bear Creek.

Dial Rock or Cambell's Ledge painted from across the Susquehanna River looking east towards Pittston.

Back Mountain winter landscape.

USGS topographical map showing the geological boundaries of the present Luzerne County.

Introduction

Land of Contrasts

"The Old Academy" housed many religious groups and provided the early community of Plymouth with a common school house.

The Van Runk store, Shickshinny, 1894.

The Old Ransom House was owned by Captain Samuel Ransom of the Second Independent Company in the Revolutionary War. His recruits numbered 84, most of which were residents of Plymouth.

Unity and diversity appear to be a contradiction in terms. However, these two forces have combined to shape the history of Luzerne County. Social, economic, political and geographic diversity challenged the people of the region long before the official establishment of Luzerne County in 1786. But through conflict and compromise a common ground was often found which allowed the county to progress and develop even in periods of great adversity. Consequently, unity was often achieved during critical periods despite the diverse nature of Luzerne County.

Social diversity is a hallmark of Luzerne County. Visible signs of the county's many cultures and ethnic groups are everywhere. In the outlying areas the well-maintained dairy farms and white clapboard churches meet new suburban developments. In the former coal towns the vestiges of the various ethnic groups are particularly striking in the hundreds of churches and fraternal organizations established to retain their heritage. Over thirty ethnic groups settled in these towns and each made their own special contribution to the region's story.

There are also clear signs of the county's economic diversity. The small but neatly kept homes in the former coal towns reflect the efforts of hard-working miners who sought to raise their economic status. Nearby, the opulent mansions that once housed the coal barons stand in sharp contrast. The affluent suburbs that have developed during the past half-century reveal the presence of a viable and growing middle class. Neatly kept farms and homes are frequently seen in the rural regions. In the midst of them, however, poverty is also found. In the crowded urban areas, the small for-

"A revelation in miners' homes" published by the Lehigh & Wilkes-Barre Coal Co. in 1923 showing the well maintained miners' homes during the yearly garden & landscaping contest in Sugar Notch.

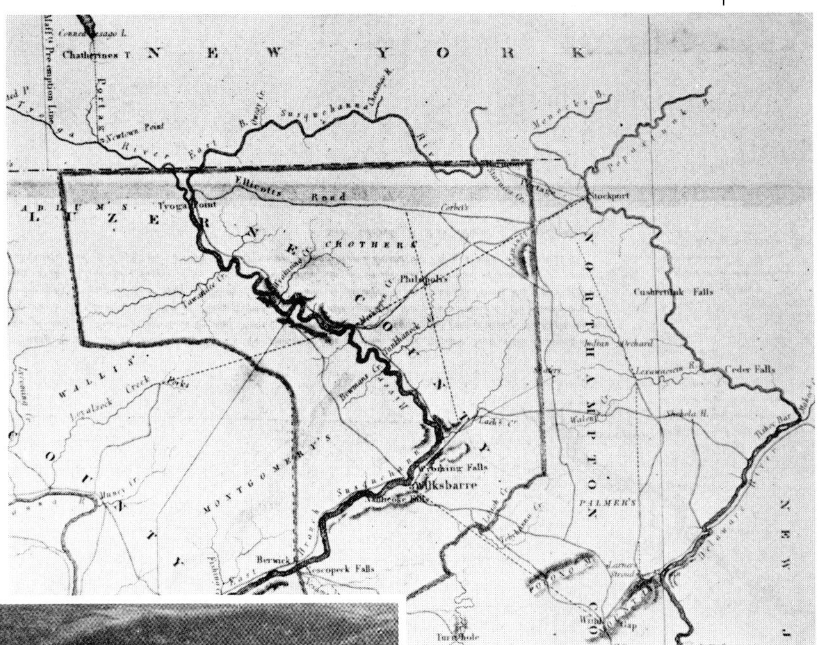

A map published in 1791 showing the original boundaries of Luzerne county shortly after its founding in 1786.

Early view of farming along the Susquehanna River taken along the original Sullivan Trail near Wyalusing, which was once part of Luzerrne County.

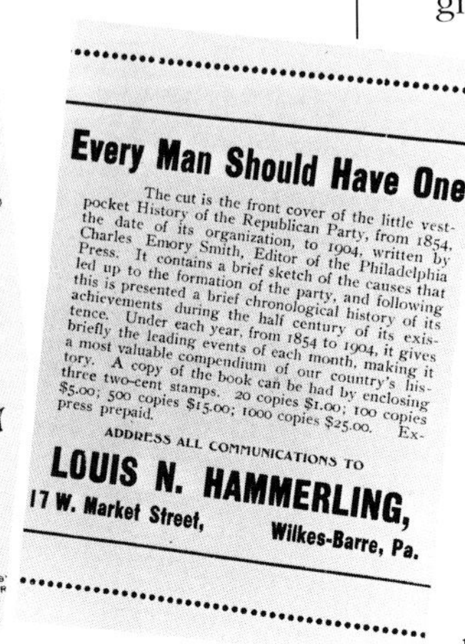

An early political advertisement soliciting sales of this pamphlet in Wilkes-Barre.

mer coal towns, and the isolated rural hills there are clear indications that some people still suffer from economic want.

Less visibly evident, but nonetheless important for understanding the county's past, is its political diversity. Luzerne County's political territory was challenged by the breaking off of four new splinter counties. In addition, political divisions existed between Wyoming Valley and the Hazleton area, prompting some Hazletonians to seek, unsuccessfully, separation into their own county. The more usual party rivalries and factions, such as blue-collar Democrats versus rural and suburban Republicans, have also been part of the local political scene throughout the twentieth century.

The history of Luzerne County is directly related to its diverse geography. Land usage determined the economic systems that have evolved. These include coal mining, dairy farming, vegetable and fruit farming, manufacturing, lumbering, and commercial and business enterprises. Consequently different geographic sub-cultures have developed in the county as a result of geographic utilization.

Such diversity can result in conflict. Social, economic, political, and geographic differences have brought about violent confrontations throughout Luzerne County's history. The region has experienced friction between rural and urban residents, various religious groups, different geographic sections, Native Americans and Europeans and their descendants, whites and minorities, labor and management, and the wealthy and the less fortunate. Yet with all this diversity, Luzerne County has attempted to find ways to compromise and accommodate these broad differences among its people and their lifestyles. Not all the solutions were fair, and at times the results caused more problems. But for the past three centuries the diverse cultures of Luzerne County have worked together for the betterment of the area. More often than not they have been successful.

Apple pickers on the Wesley Lewis farm in Exeter Township around 1900.

Luzerne County is physically divided into two major areas—the Allegheny Plateau and the Appalachian Ridge and Valley Region. The Allegheny Plateau encompasses the northern one-third of the county, while the Ridge and Valley Region takes up the southern two-thirds. The Susquehanna River bisects the county, flowing from northeast to southwest. The county's contour varies from steep, forested highlands, to rolling hills, to valley regions.

The Allegheny Plateau region is the most rugged area in the county. The term "plateau" is used to describe the rock formation, not the contour of the land. As is common in the Midwest, the rocks are laid flat upon each other rather than in the tilted formation of the Ridge and Valley region. The Allegheny Plateau can be divided into two subdivisions in the county. Extending from the northwest, three-quarters of the area consists of high plateau. The northeastern quarter is made up of low plateau.

The Ridge and Valley region is comprised of a series of parallel ridges and valleys that were eroded from the folded rock. The ridges are made up of hard sandstone, while many of the val-

The original F.W. Woolworth store was located in Seneca, New York. It was founded by Wilkes-Barre resident F.M. Kirby. It is "the oldest 5¢ &10¢ store in the world," claimed the Wilkes-Barre Independent in 1924.

AN OVERVIEW OF LUZERNE COUNTY

Luzerne County occupies 892 square miles in the lower northeastern section of Pennsylvania. The 1990 United States Census found 321,547 people residing in Luzerne County. Seventy-six incorporated municipalities are self-governing bodies. These range in population from Wilkes-Barre with 46,252 residents, to Jeddo with only 120 people. In area, Bear Creek Township is the largest with 66.4 square miles, while tiny Jeddo occupies only .125 square miles. Besides these incorporated municipalities, there are well over one-hundred subdivisions, towns and villages, which do not have self-governing powers. These include recently developed communities, some numbering over a thousand people, located in the suburban and rural townships, old rural villages, and "coal patch" towns, where only a few houses and perhaps a church are still utilized. All of these municipalities and the villages within them are served by the administrative and judicial offices located in Wilkes-Barre, the county seat.

Aerial view of Hazard Wire & Rope Manufacturing Company in Wilkes-Barre.

An aerial view of Glen Lyon showing the area's former dependence on coal mining as evidenced by the surrounding churches and close proximity of the homes and schools to the colliery.

leys have a large concentration of anthracite, or hard coal. This valuable commodity, whose presence determined much of the area's economic development, was formed during the mountain-building of the Allegheny Orogeny, 250 million years ago. Our northeastern Pennsylvania is the only area in the United States where this clean burning and efficient fuel is found in any marketable quantity.

Glaciers covered about eighty percent of Luzerne County. Only the southern tip of the county escaped the last ice age, which ended about 15,000 years ago. Glaciers helped form the Susquehanna River and the many small streams that flow through the county, creating a poor to fair quality of soil. The best soil is in the valley regions, but because of the extensive coal mining this farmland was never developed to its full potential. Most of the vegetation in the county consists of Appalachian Oak Forest, or tall broadleaf deciduous. In some of the highland areas the broadleaf and needleleaf evergreens of the Northern Hardwood Forest dominate.

The climate is generally typical of the northeastern temperate region. The average annual temperature ranges between forty-eight and fifty degrees. In January the mean temperature is between twenty-four and twenty-six degrees, while in July the average is between seventy and seventy-two degrees. Precipitation ranges between thirty-eight and forty-two inches per year while annual snowfall averages from forty to fifty inches.

Luzerne County consists of six rather separate cultural regions. These are harder to define than the geographic areas, but each of these sections had a distinct historical development. These include the Back Mountain region; Wyoming Valley; the Western Poconos; Mountaintop; the Hazleton area; and

THE FORMATION OF ANTHRACITE

The vast deposits of coal found throughout the Commonwealth are the product of fossilized plant and animal life. During the Pennsylvanian geological era, what became Pennsylvania was located near the earth's equator. Its abundance and variety of life first developed into peat, then to lignite or brown coal and eventually into bituminous, the soft coal which is found in great quantity in western Pennsylvania.

In northeastern Pennsylvania, however, the process went one step further. When the Allegheny Orogeny mountain-building stage occurred near the end of the Pennsylvanian era, the forces that folded the earth compressed the coal to an even greater degree. As a result of this pressure anthracite was formed, acquiring the highest carbon level of any type of coal. Consequently, anthracite is the cleanest and most efficiently burned of the coal fuels, and for over a century was the economic lifeblood of Luzerne County.

Author Paul Chrastina states that while seven billion tons of anthracite have been mined, over twenty billion tons still remain underground. However, because of the expense, hazards, and environmental problems faced in extraction, it is unlikely that large scale mining operations will be revived.

the Northwest Highlands and Susquehanna Valley. Each one of these sections, in varying degrees, looks to Wilkes-Barre as the central city. However, because of different geography and culture, each section has its own identity.

Located in the northern and northeastern part of the county and centered around Dallas, is the Back Mountain. Here farming once dominated the economy along with the resort of Harvey's Lake. The majority of the people were of Yankee heritage, the Methodist religion, and Republican politics. To many, they were the representation of conservative American rural values. Today in the Back Mountain area, suburban developments have replaced farmlands. It is the fastest growing area of Luzerne County, with hundreds of professionals settling in affluent neighborhoods. The area has also seen a business boom that caters to the needs and recreational activities of these new residents. Some tensions have arisen between the old rural families and the new suburban dwellers over development, community services, and taxes. However, the economic upswing brought about by the rapid growth has helped to ease the situation. To the north and east of Dallas the low plateau is still used for agriculture. Here, fruit orchards and some dairy farms are most common. This area represents both the American agricultural past and the more recent age of automobiles and suburbs.

The population center of Luzerne County has always been Wyoming Valley. Here, the cultural richness of the county is abundantly displayed, not only in the different sub-sections of the valley, centered in Pittston, the West Side, Wilkes-Barre, and Nanticoke, but also within each individual community. The region consists of a three to six mile wide area on both sides of the Susquehanna River extending about seventeen miles from north of Pittston to south of Nanticoke. It is an area of many small- to medium-sized former coal towns forming an

Dallas Methodist Episcopal Church in Dallas Township, 1885.

Back Mountain area around 1960 showing Dallas Township (left) and Shavertown (bottom).

View of Pittston around 1960 looking northeast toward West Pittston.

1960s view of Wilkes-Barre and the West Side.

almost continuous population area and crowded into the relatively level valley.

Wyoming Valley has seen a procession of different ethnic groups reflected in its culture. The area's rich ethnic heritage is visible on almost every block in the valley's wide variety of churches and clubs, and in the surnames of local businesses. Evidence of the valley's long domination by the coal industry is still visible today, thirty years after the demise of "King Coal," in abandoned mine buildings and surviving culm banks—the waste product of coal mining—as well as in some of the beautiful homes from that era which characterize Wilkes-Barre's Historic District. Signs of modernization and progress are also plentiful, such as the lovely downtown area centered on Wilkes-Barre's Public Square and a number of new housing developments. The large population and economic importance of Wyoming Valley has made it the cultural, economic, and governmental center of Luzerne County. The valley is a reflection of America's great industrial era and the challenges associated with the end of that age.

Southeast of Wyoming Valley and up Wyoming Mountain is the western gateway to the Pocono Mountains. Rising to over two thousand feet above sea level, this was once an isolated highland region settled by Yankees and by both English- and German-speaking Pennsylvanians. Throughout the 1800s, most residents farmed the rocky hillsides, while White Haven became a coal transporting town. The area experienced a boom in the late 1800s and early 1900s, when the need for support timbers in the mines made the region's lumber a valuable commodity. After this period, the western Poconos settled again into a quiet woodland area. In the post World War II era, however, the region was pulled into the Pocono Mountain vacation business. Today, thousands of tourists enjoy its recreational facilities and an increasing number of newcomers are constructing homes. New economic opportunities have brought rapid change, creating a concern for the native population.

Over the next ridge westward from the Pocono region lies Mountaintop. Located at the summits of Penobscot Mountain and Nescopeck Mountain, the area is a series of high rolling hills and valleys. The rugged terrain and generally poor soil kept the population quite small during most of the county's history. The many churches with German Protestant roots attest to the fact that the majority of the early settlers were from southeastern Pennsylvania, those Pennsylvania-Germans often referred to as "Pennsylvania Dutch" (or "Deutsche," the Germans' name for themselves) from southeastern Pennsylvania. Following World War II, a major transformation occurred in Mountaintop. With the building of the Crestwood Industrial Park, and the completion of Interstate Highways 80 and 81, Mountaintop began to boom. Today, the quiet farms have been replaced by suburban housing developments and high-tech industrial facilities. With the influx of thousands of new residents, Mountaintop, to perhaps an even greater extent than the Back Mountain, has lost many of the connections with its past.

The Hazleton area has many similarities to Wyoming Valley. As in the valley, it was the coal industry that expanded the economy, with the similar result of

Aerial photograph of Kingston in the 1960s showing suburban development.

View of the Triangle Area in Mountaintop around 1960.

View of Drums showing the farming communities still in operation between Mountaintop and Hazleton.

View of the Hazleton area around 1960 showing current and former mining operations.

creating a wide variety of ethnic groups and economic classes. However, Hazleton is a distinct part of the county. Located on a high plateau twenty-five miles from Wilkes-Barre, Hazleton is over 1,700 feet above sea level and is the highest city in Pennsylvania, while nearby Freeland is the state's highest borough. The mountains that formed a geographic separation also created a cultural separation from Wyoming Valley. Hazletonians have often had strong connections with the coal towns in the southern anthracite region, and at times have not been comfortable with the influence exerted by Wyoming Valley in county affairs. Past efforts to form a separate county in the Hazleton area illustrate the position taken by those who believe that the region has been neglected by the power brokers in Wilkes-Barre.

The Hazleton area in lower Luzerne County has a different appearance than Wyoming Valley. In Wyoming Valley coal companies most often operated in towns that were already organized entities. Many of the Hazleton area towns, however, were "company towns." Founded by the coal companies, they had greater distances between them, and took on the look of "patch towns."

Although coal production in the Hazleton area continued longer than in Wyoming Valley, it was lower Luzerne County that took the lead in economic recovery. The CAN-DO industrial development organization served as a model for community-based revitalization programs. The Hazleton area today is a combination of modern suburbs and industrial plants mixed with the old company towns and strip mine operations. Recently the county's two former coal regions have cooperated more, although the Hazleton area still desires to maintain its distinctive nature.

The Northwest Highlands and Susquehanna Valley region consists mainly of rural areas in western Luzerne County that are part of the river's watershed. This area was most separated from the coal culture. The landscape rises from the river valley to North Mountain in the north and to Nescopeck Mountain along the southern boundary. At nearly 2,500 feet these mountains are the highest points in Luzerne County. The people have often looked downriver to Berwick, in

View of the Hazleton area showing downtown around 1960.

Columbia County, as their central city. Their history has been linked to frontier and rural life. Farmers, hunters, and loggers played dominant roles in the region's development, and today dairy farms are set among the vast woodlands. In recent times, the highland areas have been a haven for sportsmen and vacationers. The river valley economy expanded following the building of the Pennsylvania Power and Light Company's Susquehanna nuclear power plant. Still the region remains the most rural area of the county. The Northwest Highlands and Susquehanna Valley region serves as a vivid example of small-town and rural life, once the dominate culture in American history.

In view of the diversity in Luzerne County, one may wonder how any sense of unity could prevail. History demonstrates that it was never an easy task. There were many struggles to reach common goals and to understand each other. But despite the struggles, the historical process moved towards unity rather than fragmentation. In many ways the county has been a microcosm of America. The parallels are striking. Such phenomenon as European encroachment on Native Americans, the rural ideal, industrialization, immigration, economic successes and failures, and cultural diversity have all been a part of both American and Luzerne County history. Like the nation, Luzerne County has sought to achieve unity while maintaining diversity.

A TOUR OF LUZERNE COUNTY

Driving through Luzerne County with the assistance of a county map can provide an overview of its history and culture. Begin on Route 29, at the border of Luzerne and Wyoming counties. One mile south is Harvey's Lake, the largest in volume of Pennsylvania's natural lakes. Proceed south on Route 415 to Dallas. There, take any secondary road eastward through the rolling hills of the Back Mountain to see the new suburbs and the older farms and fruit orchards.

Eventually these roads lead to Route 92. Go south on it along the Susquehanna River to U.S. 11 in West Pittston. Or cross the Susquehanna and drive south on the east side of the river. Wyoming Valley's diversity is visible in the architecture of its churches, commercial buildings, and homes. At the northern and southern ends of the valley are Pittston and Nanticoke. These cities and their surrounding towns are showcases for the still strong ethnic culture. In Wilkes-Barre, in the valley's center, are both the opulent county courthouse and the modern downtown area, as well as the campuses of Wilkes University and King's College. Kingston, both independent town and Wilkes-Barre suburb, lies directly across the river.

Take Route 115 south over Wyoming Mountain to the western fringes of the Pocono Mountain resort region. In this area many of the older farms have given way to suburban communities and vacation homes. After arriving in White Haven take Route 437 north into Mountaintop. Proceed southward along Route 309 through a bustling suburban area with a large industrial park at its center.

Route 309 continues over Appalachian ridges and valleys to Hazleton, an area rich in mining history with many small coal patches. The Hazleton area combines this ethnic coal mining tradition with modern industrial and commercial centers.

Leave the Hazleton area by Route 93 north. This pleasant drive through the mountains will bring one to the Susquehanna River in Nescopeck. After crossing the river go north to Ricketts Glen State Park. Route 487 winds up North Mountain, the highest point in Luzerne County.

At a leisurely pace this journey through Luzerne County can take the best part of a day. In the process the traveler will see not only the full spectrum of the county's geography, but also a wide variety of Luzerne County's culture and history.

Fishing in remote country streams, made possible by motorcycle transportation.

CHAPTER ONE

Archeologist Max Schrabisch in 1924 atop the Kelly Ridge rock shelter on Wyoming Mountain where he excavated evidence of its use as a prehistoric campsite.

People of the Woodlands and Frontier

Native American implements found between Pittston and Berwick by local archeologists from 1884 to 1902. The central image was unearthed at a Native American burial site on Boston Hill in Plymouth Township in 1888.

Leaden images of Roman Catholic icons set in plaster molds, and a brass crucifix, found in Native American excavations in the Wyoming Valley.

Archeological excavations indicate that the first inhabitants of the region that became Luzerne County hunted near the Susquehanna River approximately 12,000 years ago. Little is known about these nomadic hunters other than the discovery of their Clovis-style spear points near present-day Duryea. The earliest evidence of permanent settlement in the county is estimated at 980 A.D., using radiocarbon dating of artifacts found at the excavation of the Airport II site in Forty Fort.

These early residents lived in villages and supplemented their hunting, fishing, and gathering by cultivating some corn. To date, six sites indicating permanent settlement have been discovered in Wyoming Valley. Some are heavily stockaded, and were occupied during a later period when their inhabitants' diets relied chiefly on the cultivation of corn. By 1575 these villages had been abandoned. Some scholars speculate that war or disease may have been responsible, while others theorize that changing economic conditions drove the inhabitants away.

By 1675 the Iroquois Confederacy, centered in upstate New York, had gained control of present-day Luzerne County. The Delaware called this region "Maugh-wau-wa-me," meaning large plains, and the region became known as "Wyoming" to the English. It was, to the Iroquois, the southern entrance or gateway to their territory, which they referred to as their longhouse. However, the Iroquois did not have the necessary numbers to settle the area. To protect their claim to the land they invited displaced tribes to reside in the valley. The Shawnee, Mahicans, Mohegans, Lenni Lenape (who became known as the Delaware), Tuscarora, and Nanticoke all took advantage of this offer.

The Shawnee were the first of these tribes to settle on the Iroquois land. They established a village near present-day Plymouth in 1701. The Mahicans also resided on the Shawnee Flats while the Mohegans settled on the upper Kingston Flats. The Nanticoke established a village in the town that today bears their name, while the Tuscarora are thought to have made their homes in what is now the Pittston area. The Lenni Lenape (Delaware) established at least two villages along the river and occupied some land in what is now the southeastern corner of the county.

Throughout the first half of the

Forty Fort in 1788.

Fort Wyoming in Wilkes-Barre in 1771-1774.

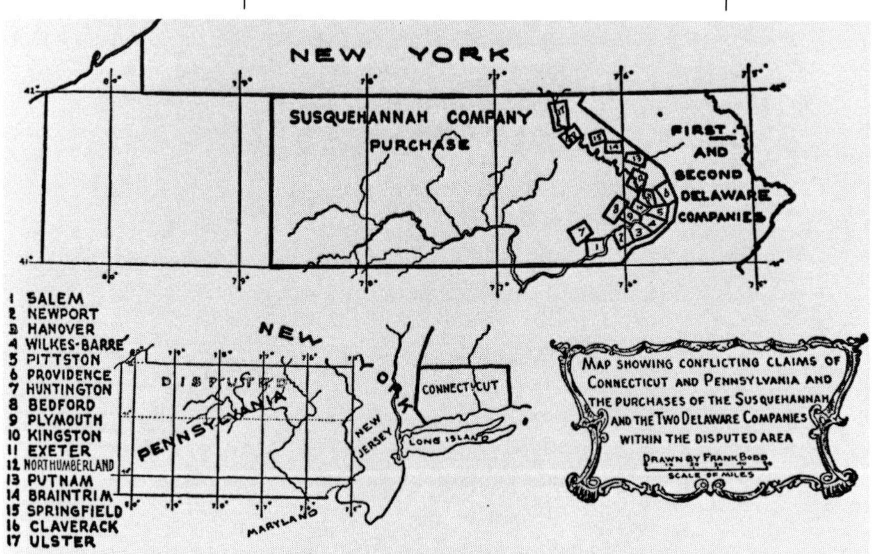

Map showing Connecticut Townships set-up in Wyoming Valley.

A map showing the migration of Connecticut Yankees to the North Branch of the Susquehanna River.

18th century these tribes farmed the flatland and hunted in the nearby hills. However, they faced increasing disruption as the descendants of the seaboard European settlers moved westward.

Between 1730 and 1753 the population of the Connecticut colony tripled. As a result, farmland was at a premium and colonists began to look westward for new areas to settle. In 1683 Connecticut's original western claim was abrogated by New York. The Yankees saw the frontier land of the Susquehanna River valley as the next logical step in their westward migration, and in 1753 they organized the Susquehannah Company as a means of promoting its settlement.

Two major obstacles stood in their way. First, the Onondaga Council of the Iroquois had claimed this region since 1575. The British, who were profiting from the fur trade in the Susquehanna region, generally supported the Iroquois' rights to the area. Secondly, the charter that British King Charles II had granted to the Penn family in 1681 gave Pennsylvania a solid claim to the area.

The Susquehannah Company, however, was determined to settle Wyoming. An agent of the company, John Henry Lydius, began to secure the signatures of some of the Mohawk chiefs, whose tribe was one of Six Nations of the Iroquois. These signatures were used to show Iroquoian authorization for the Connecticut claim to the land. The legality of this land acquisition was questionable. In the first place, the signers were not official representatives of the Six Nations, and had no right to sign over the land. Also it was reported that they were persuaded to sign with the help of rum. Nonetheless, the Connecticut Yankees insisted that, through Lydius, they had acquired the right to settle the land.

In 1762, the first English settlement in what would become Luzerne County was established. Approximately one hundred Connecticut Yankees settled at the

COUNT VON ZINZENDORF

Nicolaus Ludwig, Count von Zinzendorf, was born in Saxony in 1700. At age 27 he organized the emigrants to Saxony from Moravia and Bohemia into the Church of the Brethren, forerunner of the United Brethren or Moravian Church in America. Consecrated bishop in 1737, Zinzendorf went to America in 1741 to inspect the Moravian establishments and to learn about their work among the Indians. He was described, on a visit to the Philadelphia area that year, by the Hon. James Logan: "He speaks Latin and French,...wears his own hair and is in all other respects very plain as making the propagation of the Gospel his whole purpose and business."

On arrival at the Forks of the Delaware (where the Lehigh joins the Delaware River) just before Christmas 1741, Zinzendorf named the new Moravian settlement there Bethlehem. That city has been the headquarters of the Moravian Church in America ever since.

On October 13th, 1742, after a dangerous and fatiguing journey, Count Zinzendorf, Anna Nitschmann, John Martin Mack and his wife, Jeannette, guided by Andrew Montour, arrived at Wyoming, then the name of the Shawnee village in what is now Plymouth. It consisted of thirty or forty cabins, about one and a quarter miles from a small Mahican town upriver. On October 22nd, they were joined by David Nitschmann, Anton Seyffert, and Jacob Kohn, and a few days later by Pennsylvania's Indian Agent, Conrad Weiser, who had been worried by the party's long absence.

Unlike the Delaware and other Wyoming Valley inhabitants, many of whom were to become Moravian converts to Christianity, the Shawnee were, in Zinzendorf's opinion, a "perfidious race and desired no knowledge of God and the Savior." In fact, the Shawnee suspected the missionaries of wanting to take their land. Weiser was concerned for the missionaries' lives, and was relieved when the party left Wyoming Valley for Bethlehem on November 1st.

Zinzendorf left for England in January 1743. He died in 1760 at Herrnhut, his estate in Saxony. Among his voluminous writings were two hymns he composed entitled, "Wayomik Im November 1742," written during his visit to this area.

Most of the Shawnee living in Wyoming Valley at the time of Zinzendorf's visit moved to Ohio in 1744. The remainder left the valley in 1756, first moving northward, then west to Ohio.

---

confluence of Mill Creek and the Susquehanna River. Today, this site is near the Wilkes-Barre Cemetery on North River Street. Despite warnings from the Indians, the colony of Pennsylvania, and the British government, the Yankees erected some log houses, a gristmill, and a sawmill. They returned to Connecticut for the winter of 1762-1763, but came back to Wyoming when spring arrived.

On April 19, 1763 the situation turned violent. Teedyuscung, chief of the Delawares in Wyoming Valley, had complained to the Pennsylvania government about the encroachment of the settlers. The chief's Pennsylvania-built cabin and some other homes were burned to the ground. Teedyuscung, reportedly drunk and certainly sound asleep during the incident, was killed. The Yankee settlers blamed the Delaware's enemies. However, it was more likely that the settlers themselves were responsible for the death of the man they saw as a barrier to their settlement. In October of 1763, Teedyuscung's son, Captain Bull, avenged his father's death by killing twenty settlers and driving the remainder back to Connecticut. The pattern of violence, which dominated the area for the next twenty years, was just beginning.

From 1763 to 1769 the only English-speaking residents of Wyoming were Captain Amos Ogden and his associates, who had permission from the Penn family to operate a trading post. However,

Chief Teedyuscung.

AIRPORT II ARCHEOLOGICAL SITE: A VIEW OF A PRE-HISTORIC NATIVE AMERICAN VILLAGE

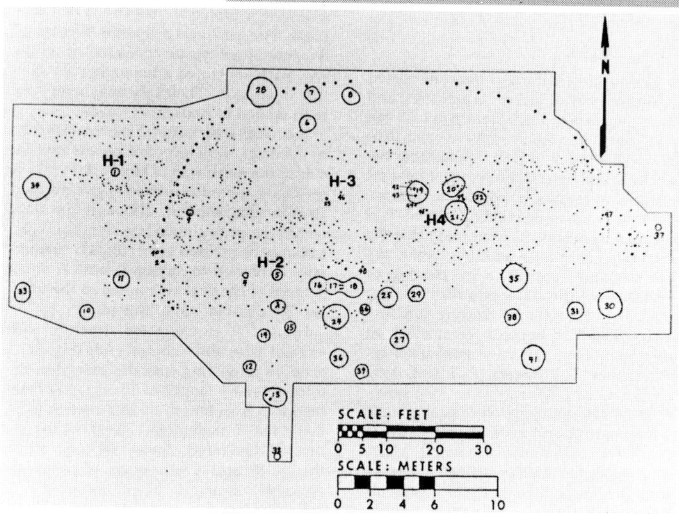

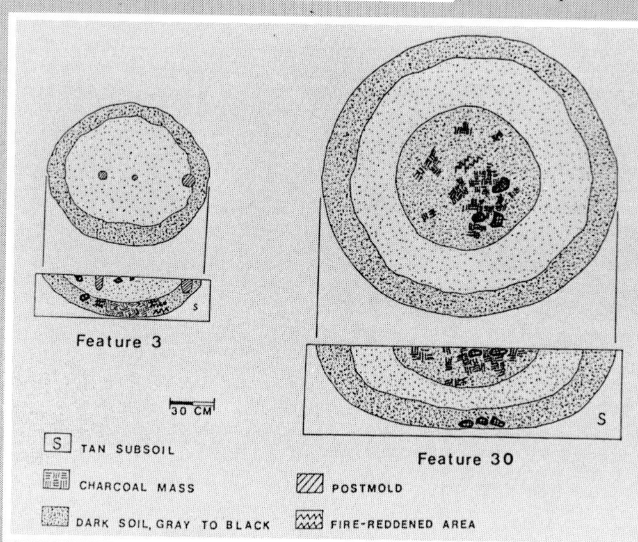

Plan view of the Airport II archeological site and pit excavations depicting structural features and probable house locations.

The Airport II archeological site was first excavated by Christopher Wren in 1914. In 1985 the site was reopened when the Frances Dorrance Chapter 11 of the Society for Pennsylvania Archeology received permission to do a dig from Forty-Fort Borough. In 1986 Francis D. Garrahan and John Orlandini proceeded with the excavation. Their findings were published by Garrahan in "A Clemson Island/Owasco Settlement on the North Branch of the Susquehanna," (*Pennsylvania Archeologist*, February, 1990).

The villagers who resided at the Airport II site had established a relatively permanent settlement at this location. According to Wyoming Valley historian Sally Teller Lottick, the villagers hunted and fished, ate nuts and mussels, and used tobacco in pipes. Most important is the evidence that they grew corn. Their involvement in agriculture indicates that they had a commitment to stay on this tract of land.

Excavations also uncovered an incomplete stockade. The purpose of this enclosure has not been fully determined. It may have been constructed as a defense fortification that at one time surrounded the whole village and was subsequently eroded by Susquehanna River flooding. Another theory is that the stockade was built to fend off severe weather and only needed to be partially completed. Remnants of such buildings as a longhouse and a pen were found both inside and outside the stockade. The villagers apparently rebuilt these structures over the years. This could mean that the site was a seasonal residence or that the villagers were involved in regular maintenance of the original construction work.

Archeologists are continuing excavations at sites throughout Luzerne County. Through the support of the Society for Pennsylvania Archeology, Frances Dorrance Chapter 11, additional insights into the lives of the county's first residents can be gained.

1769 saw the competition for the land intensify. The Penn family, anxious to protect their northern lands, sent civil and military authorities to Wyoming. Called Pennamites, they were led by Captain Ogden, Sheriff John Jennings, and Charles Stewart. The group agreed to maintain the Wyoming trading post and constructed Fort Ogden near Mill Creek. In exchange for their services they were granted tenancies on the Manors of Stoke and Sunbury, the two large tracts of land into which the Penns had divided the Wyoming area.

Three weeks after the Pennamites came to Wyoming, the first forty Connecticut settlers, for whom Forty Fort was later named, arrived in Wyoming. The Pennamites immediately attempted to demonstrate who was in charge. Sheriff Jennings arrested Major John Durkee, the Yankee leader. He was sent to Easton for trial. However, due to some bureaucratic bungling over who had jurisdiction, Durkee was released and returned to Wyoming. In April 1769, two hundred more Yankees settled in the valley. Durkee was elected president, and the pioneers erected Fort Durkee on the river bank between present-day South and Ross Streets. They also established five settling townships—Wilkes-Barre, Nanticoke (later Hanover), Plymouth, Forty-Fort (later Kingston), and Pittston.

These rival claims for Wyoming Valley led to the Yankee-Pennamite Wars. The first open conflict began in November 1769. The Pennamites again captured Major Durkee and sent him to Philadelphia. Then, under the direction of Sheriff Jennings, a Pennamite posse two hundred strong and aided in their efforts by a newly acquired cannon, proceeded to rout the Yankee settlements.

The Pennamite advantage was short-lived. Yankee Captain Zebulon Butler enlisted the aid of Lazarus Stewart and his Paxtang Boys. These Scots-Irish Presbyterians were renowned Indian fighters and no friends of the Pennsylvania government. The Paxtang Boys lived up to their reputation and took Fort Wyoming on April 2, 1770. The Yankees were victorious in the First Yankee-Pennamite War, and Stewart and the Paxtang Boys were granted "a good township of six miles square"—Nanticoke Township, which they renamed Hanover.

The period between 1770 and the American Revolution was peaceful in Wyoming. The Yankees developed their settlements. The township surveys were completed. Wilkes-Barre was laid out on the east side of the Susquehanna River, and on the west side the Great Road, now present-day Wyoming Avenue, was surveyed and the town of Forty Fort was laid out. On June 29, 1774, the entire region, appropriately called Westmoreland, became a town in Litchfield County, Connecticut, nearly two hundred miles to the east.

Despite the outbreak of the American Revolution, Yankee-Pennamite hostilities were renewed at the Battle of Rampart Rocks near present-day West Nanticoke. A Pennamite force of six hundred, led by Northumberland County's presiding judge, Colonel William Plunkett, was defeated by the Yankees on Christmas day, 1775. The Yankee victory led the Connecticut assembly to create Westmoreland County, with a population of about 2,000, out of the former town of Westmoreland.

On April 15, 1776, both Yankees and Pennamites agreed to honor a Continental Congress resolution to cease fighting each other. The warfare that replaced the Yankee-Pennamite conflict, however, became etched in the minds of the settlers for the next two centuries.

The three groups competing for the Wyoming Valley—Yankee, Pennamite, and Iroquois—looked at the conflict from different perspectives. After the Battle of Bunker Hill, the Yankees in Westmoreland voted to "unanimously join their brethren in America in the common cause of defending their liberty." They formed the 24th Regiment with Zebulon Butler as colonel. The positions of the Pennamites varied. Some fought for the Revolutionary cause, believing that their claim would be upheld by a future American court. Others favored Great Britain, thinking that the British courts were more likely to support their claim to Westmoreland. The Iroquois, already bilked of their lands in northeastern Pennsylvania, had the best reason for supporting the British. Great Britain was very likely to recognize the Iroquois claim to the lands west of the Appalachian Mountains. Most of the Six Nations

A benevolent relationship between the first settlers and the Native American inhabitants.

Battle of Rampart Rocks.

Illustration depicting the story of Queen Esther's revenge for the death of her son following the Battle of Wyoming.

Farms in Wyoming Valley being looted and burned by the Indian allies of the British following the Battle of Wyoming.

Completed in 1843, the Wyoming Monument provides a tomb for the bones of those killed in the July 3, 1778, Battle of Wyoming.

believed that the Americans, anxious for westward expansion, would not be sympathetic to the Native American concerns.

In June of 1778, approximately seven hundred Tories, Rangers, and Native Americans organized at Fort Wintermoot. Leading these pro-British forces, including Chief Sayenqueraghta's Senecas, was Major John Butler.

Scouting parties told the Americans about the military build-up and they took what seemed to be the appropriate course of action. The families of the 24th Regiment gathered in the forts for protection, while the military unit marched from Forty Fort on July 3, 1778. This force of 375 carried the Stars and Stripes of the new American nation and marched to the fife and drum playing "St. Patrick's Day in the Morning." They were led by Colonel Zebulon Butler with Colonel Nathan Denison as second-in-command.

The original plan was to hold at Abraham's Creek until reinforcements arrived. However, unaware of the size of the enemy forces, Lazarus Stewart and others demanded that the troops press on to meet the enemy. Zebulon Butler, despite being an experienced officer in Washington's army, was overruled, and the soldiers marched three miles northward to the Exeter flats.

The decision to confront the enemy may have been a demonstration of American bravery, but from a military standpoint it was foolhardy. The superior British force routed the Americans in about thirty minutes to claim victory in the Battle of Wyoming. Nearly two hundred settlers lost their lives compared to about eighty of the Tories, Rangers, and Native Americans. That evening sixteen or eighteen captured colonials were tortured and killed. The story circulated to the American and British public regarding this Wyoming Massacre was that an Indian woman, perhaps Queen Esther Montour, danced around a rock upon which the captives were held, and with maul and tomahawk, killed them.

In the late afternoon hours of July 4, 1778, Colonel Denison surrendered Wyoming Valley to the British. The Native Americans burned and looted the settlements, effectively destroying their potential as a food source for the American army. However, the British Major John Butler made a strong effort to see that the defeated survivors were spared. The settlers were exiled to the south, while the British forces moved northward. Once again, Wyoming Valley was unoccupied.

The Battle of Wyoming had important consequences for Luzerne County. The short-term effect was a retaliatory campaign aimed at destroying the Iroquois's farm economy as a supply source for the British army. In the spring of 1779, George Washington ordered General John Sullivan and 3,500 troops to achieve the "total destruction and

FRANCES SLOCUM

Four months after the Battle of Wyoming, on November 2, 1778, the Slocum farm was hit in a quick raid by a small party of Indians. The farm was located on the northern edge of the settlement of Wilkes-Barre, about where Frances Slocum Playground now stands at the corner of North Street and Pennsylvania Avenue. Five-year old Frances Slocum was kidnapped by the raiding party, along with another child. She disappeared, and despite their long, hard search, her family did not see her again until 1837, almost sixty years later.

Frances was carried over the mountains by the raiding party, and on arrival at a village that may have been Fort Niagara, her captor, a Delaware chief named Tuck Horse, dressed her in the Indian way and took her to be adopted by an old man and woman of his tribe who had lost all their children. They brought her up as their own child, and when her first husband, also a Delaware, moved on west, she elected to stay and take care of her adoptive parents instead of going with him. Her second husband was Shepconah, a Miami brave, whose life she saved.

After her second marriage, Frances became a member of the Miami tribe, taking the name Maconaqua. After 1815, when Shepconah retired as war chief, the couple and their children moved upstream along the Mississineva River to what became known as Deaf Man's Village.

The Slocum family located Frances through a letter to the Lancaster *Intelligencer* written by Col. George W. Ewing, in which he related Maconaqua's history. She had told him the story of her early life one evening, when he was sheltering in Maconaqua's cabin and she was feeling ill,

When the Slocums found Frances, they wanted her to come back and live with them. But she felt that for most of her life she had been an Indian and she and her children were where they belonged. Nor could she persuade her brother to stay and make his home with her. But they became close, and eventually one of her nephews and his family joined her in her village.

Frances Slocum/Maconaqua was a remarkable woman, successfully bridging two very different cultures and her two very different families.

A portrait of Frances Slocum painted in 1839 and a scene depicting her capture.

Major John Durkee, leader of the Connecticut settlers.

General John Sullivan, 1740-1795, leader of the 1779 expedition against the Iroquois.

devastation of their (Iroquois) settlements, and the capture of as many prisoners of every age and sex as possible." Sullivan's March resulted in the burning of forty Indian villages and the ravaging of their farmlands. The Native American population in the upper Susquehanna Valley was forcibly uprooted.

Some settlers returned to Wilkes-Barre within a few months of the Battle of Wyoming. It was Sullivan's March in 1779 that secured the area under colonial control as the bulk of the Revolutionary War fighting moved to the South. The Indians who claimed the area of Luzerne County were never again able to mount a large scale action against the settlers in the region. However, they did continue to harass them. For example, in 1780 a group of travelers enroute to Wilkes-Barre were attacked by a band of Indians in the vicinity of Sugarloaf Mountain. Thirteen were killed in what became known as the Sugarloaf Massacre.

As American Studies scholar Clement L. Valletta has explained, the long-term significance of the Battle of Wyoming was the myth that grew up around it. The retelling of the battle often failed to mention the reasons for the Indians' hostility, the inept military tactics of the colonial forces, the enemy commander's decision to prevent further bloodshed after the battle, and General Sullivan's destruction of forty Indian villages. Instead, the heroic efforts of the soldiers, who fought and died for the Revolutionary cause and to protect their homes and families, became the stuff of legend and a source of great pride to their descendants.

The American victory over the British in 1781 renewed the dispute between Connecticut and Pennsylvania over northeastern Pennsylvania. In 1782, Congress commissioned five men to decide which state had the rightful claim to the land. They issued the Decree of Trenton which unanimously ruled that the "state of Connecticut has no right to the Lands in Controversy," and the Commonwealth of Pennsylvania held the "Right" of ownership to the region. Westmoreland County ceased to exist, and the area became a part of Northumberland County, Pennsylvania.

Once the decree was issued, Pennsylvania ruled that the Yankee settlers were not citizens of the Commonwealth. Therefore, the Yankees could not vote in elections and were to give up any property deeded to Pennsylvanians. Colonel John Franklin, a veteran of the Battle

Colonel John Franklin, 1749-1831, Yankee leader during the Second Yankee-Pennamite War.

of Wyoming, now became the leader of the angry Yankees. In exploring the options available for defending the Connecticut claims, he even proposed the establishment of a new state with Wilkes-Barre as its capital. Not wanting to relinquish Wyoming Valley, Pennsylvania organized a military unit led by Northampton County Justice of the Peace Alexander Patterson. With this, the Second Yankee-Pennamite War began. In May 1784, Patterson's troops began the forced evacuation of Yankee residents from Wyoming Valley to the Delaware River. Patterson's cruel treatment of the settlers on this sixty mile trek aroused the anger of Connecticut and Pennsylvania residents alike.

Pennsylvania then dispatched Colonel Timothy Pickering to Wyoming. This native New Englander was charged with resolving the disputed land claims. He recommended that Pennsylvania maintain ownership of the land but that Yankee property deeds held prior to the Trenton Decree be honored. The Yankees accepted this arrangement and in celebration burned Fort Wyoming. Although the Pickering proposal was eventually put into effect, it must be noted that Pennsylvania tried to renege on the initial agreement. Individual land disputes continued into the nineteenth century.

In order to achieve a measure of peace in the area, and an end to the Second Yankee-Pennamite War, the Pennsylvania Assembly proposed a compromise. On September 23, 1786, a new county was separated from Northumberland County. Both Yankee and Pennamite settlers in the area would have voting rights and a measure of self-government.

The new county was named Luzerne, in honor of Chevalier de la Luzerne, the French minister to the United States during the last years of the Revolutionary War. Wilkes-Barre became its seat. The new county included the present-day areas of Luzerne, Lackawanna, Wyoming, and Susquehanna counties, and part

Timothy Pickering came to the new Luzerne County in 1786 to resolve the land claims between Connecticut and Pennsylvania settlers.

of Bradford County. Susquehanna and Bradford counties broke away from Luzerne in 1810, while Wyoming and Lackawanna Counties formed separate governments in 1842 and 1878, respectively.

In 1790 the population of Luzerne County was only 1,904. By 1800 it numbered 12,839 people and by 1810 it had increased to 18,109. This rapid growth was county-wide. From the 1770s to the early 1800s settlements in most of the regions of present-day Luzerne County were established. Some were founded by Yankees relocating from Wyoming Valley, while others were established by pioneers arriving from New England and from southeastern Pennsylvania.

The southern fringes of Wyoming Valley were first settled in 1772 when Major Prince Alden built his home in Newport Township. By the 1770s property deeds were being granted to Connecticut settlers in locations further south in the watershed of the Susquehanna River's North Branch. Settlements were soon established in Salem Township, while across the river, Pennsylvania-Germans began to move into what is present-day Nescopeck Township.

It was Pennsylvania-Germans who were responsible for the first settlement in the Butler Valley in 1784. Led by John Balliet, many natives of

Born in Paris in 1741, Chevalier de la Luzerne adopted a military career and served in the seven years' war as a colonel. He was appointed minister to the United States in 1778, and helped with the post war distress by raising badly needed funds. Luzerne County was named for him by the Act of Sept. 25, 1786.

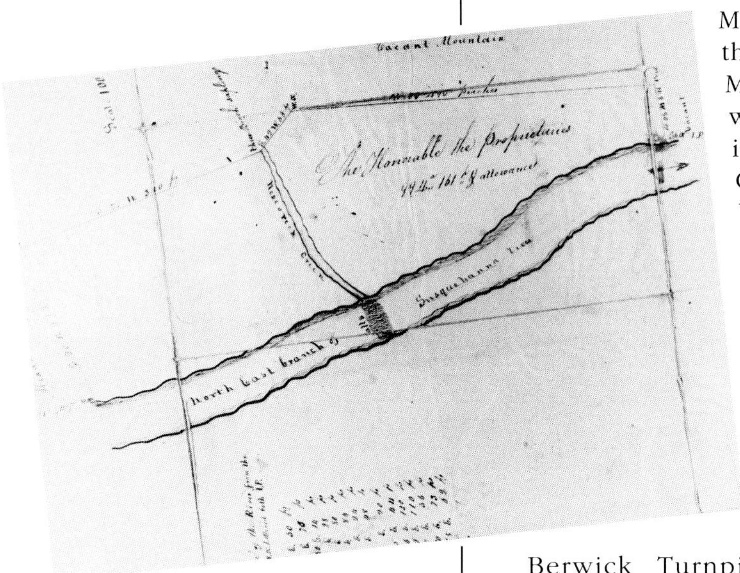

The first land survey of "Nescopeck" at the confluence of the Susquehanna River and Nescopeck Creek, by the surveyor, Charles Stewart, dated Dec. 27, 1768-Feb. 8, 1769.

Northampton County came to this region a few miles north of present-day Hazleton. Yankees migrating from Wyoming Valley's villages established the first settlements in the Back Mountain in the late 1700s. Mountaintop was first settled in 1798 by Conrad Wickeiser. Many of his fellow Germans soon made their homes in this highland region. The building of the old Berwick Turnpike in 1804 brought the first pioneers to Hazleton. Jacob Drumheller, who built a hotel along the roadway, is often credited with being the first settler there.

Since the Connecticut settlers dominated the Back Mountain area and the northern part of Wyoming Valley, the Yankee dialect and the New England style of home and barn architecture prevailed there, along with the Congregational church. Around the turn of the century several of these churches changed to a Presbyterian affiliation. Also, the Second Great Awakening religious revival resulted in large conversions to Methodism.

The lower Wyoming Valley had a more mixed population. Although the Yankees were well represented, large numbers of Scots-Irish and Pennsylvania-Germans settled there as well. The speech patterns were a mixture of Yankee and Midland accents. Barn and house architecture reflected New England, Middle Atlantic, and Pennsylvania-German styles. German-speaking Lutheran and Reformed churchgoers worshiped along with their English-speaking Presbyterian and Methodist neighbors.

The Pennsylvania-German influence was felt most strongly in the southern half of Luzerne County. Large numbers of Germans migrated from the area of present-day Schuylkill, Berks, Lehigh, and Northampton counties into Mountaintop, the Butler Valley, Nescopeck, and Hazleton. Many spoke with a Pennsylvania Dutch accent. ("Dutch" is a misinterpretation of the word "Deutsche," meaning German.) They established Lutheran and German Reformed churches, and erected structures in the Pennsylvania-German style. In addition to the Germans, English-speaking Pennsylvanians also moved into the southern portions of Luzerne County. In this region the Midland dialect was more pronounced. The New England influence, so important in Wyoming Valley and the Back Mountain, did not play as great a role in lower Luzerne County.

As the nineteenth century arrived Luzerne County was a developing area, but one that was still primarily rural. Agriculture dominated the economy and most residents were somehow connected to that occupation. At first the diversity of the people in the region led not just to conflict, but to bloodshed. The Native Americans were forced out of Wyoming Valley. Yankees and Pennamites killed each other over conflicting land claims, and both battled the British and Loyalists for control of the region. However, compromises and accommodations eventually brought a degree of harmony to the region. The establishment of the new county satisfied both the Yankee citizens and the Pennsylvania government. And the various cultural groups each established their own sphere of influence. By the coming of the new century Luzerne County had become a union of diverse people ready to face the challenge of the Industrial Age.

LIFE IN THE WYOMING VALLEY IN 1800

Wyoming Valley towns echoed the New England origins of their founders. They were designed with town squares or commons, or, like Wilkes-Barre, with both. This public land was used for grazing the town dwellers' animals. Maple trees were planted along the roadside. Homes were scattered, and with the exception of the main thoroughfares, most roads and streets were narrow dirt lanes. The houses were simple, often unpainted, and like the barns, reflected the New England style of architecture.

Most people were farmers. Other occupations were trades that supported agricultural life such as wheelwrights, harness-makers, and blacksmiths. While men managed farms or businesses, women took charge of household and barnyard duties. Large families were the norm and most chores, including making clothes, were done by hand. Few people had any wealth, and any unexpected turn of events could lead to economic disaster. When the Susquehanna River overflowed in 1784, it was reported that only the abundance of shad saved the people from starvation.

Despite the hard work the residents had a variety of amusements. The young people enjoyed occasional parties and balls. In the winter months sledding was popular. The arrival of a small circus in the summer was always greeted with excitement. Adult attention was often focused on church activities. The consumption of alcoholic beverages was common throughout all of rural Pennsylvania in 1800, and it was not until the 1840s that the temperance movement had a major impact in Luzerne County. Although liquor was necessary as a painkiller in the absence of more effective medicine, some indulged on a regular basis. H. Hollister, an early historian of the Pennsylvania-Yankees, once remarked that a "prominent and universal characteristic of the people was the love of whiskey." Whether or not this was a studied observation, one can assume that drinking was not uncommon in Wyoming Valley.

By the 1830s this agricultural society was changing. Some Yankee descendants migrated to the rich farmlands of northern Ohio's Western Reserve region. The design of the towns and the architecture of the structures in northern Ohio still reflects a strong New England connection. However, it was the growth of the anthracite industry that changed Wyoming Valley from a rural to an industrial society.

View of the Jenkins house and farm, built on a portion of land that had been the site of the Battle of Wyoming.

Wilkes-Barre Public Square showing the settlement of the county seat in Luzerne County, about 1830.

View of "Industrial Wilkes-Barre" in 1906.

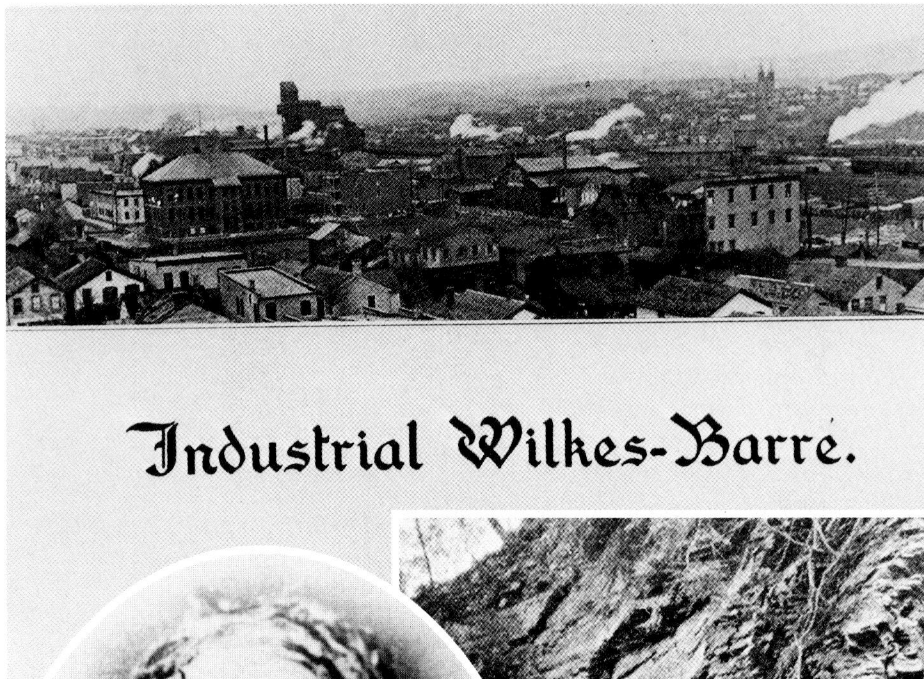

Original mining operations made by Abijah Smith in 1807 set the stage for later coal prospecting all over the anthracite field.

In 1811 coal prospector Freeman Thomas purchased the Avondale property in Plymouth, where he pushed his "grand tunnel" through the mountain rock until he reached coal. Although much more expensive than working the visible coal outcroppings, the cost was soon offset by the rewards of the new industry.

Miners with petrified tree stump, c. 1940.

C H A P T E R T W O

Builders of a New Era

Called "stone coal" by the first Europeans to enter the Wyoming Valley, this hard carbon fossil substance known as anthracite forever altered life in Luzerne County. It changed the county from a quiet frontier land into a thriving industrial support region. With it came great wealth and community development, but it was also responsible for poverty and the creation of towns divided along ethnic and religious lines. It affected not only the specific areas in which coal was mined, but also changed the relationship between town and country in Luzerne County. The period between 1800 and 1880 marked the formative years of the Industrial Revolution in Luzerne County as well as in America as a whole, and witnessed the change from a frontier to an agricultural society in the rural regions.

The potential of anthracite was recognized as early as 1760. While James Tilghman of Philadelphia traversed the banks of the Susquehanna, he found large quantities of the substance throughout Wyoming Valley. He wrote to Thomas and Richard Penn, descendants of the colonial proprietor, that coal may become "a thing of great value." The Penns were apparently not impressed. The same could be said for most of the early settlers in the region. Because of the high carbon content the coal was extremely hard, and difficult to ignite in the common fireplace grates of the period.

In 1769, by using a forced draft, blacksmiths Obadiah and Daniel Gore succeeded in firing their forge with stone coal. Soon the word spread to other smiths. Because of the intense heat produced by anthracite, it replaced charcoal as the preferred substance in forges throughout Luzerne County. Anthracite even found its way to Carlisle, Pennsylvania, were it fired the forges that produced guns for

Breaker boys and foreman in mountainside "dog hole" excavation site separating rock from coal.

An early painting of the covered bridge at Market Street in Wilkes-Barre. The bridge first replaced the ferries in 1818.

Fell Tavern.

the Revolutionary War troops.

While local blacksmiths followed the Gores' example in the forced-draft burning of anthracite, its use for home heating did not become widespread until Judge Jesse Fell of Wilkes-Barre solved the problem of igniting hard coal in a common, home-style grate. In the early years of the nineteenth century, Fell, like Oliver Evans of Philadelphia, experimented with anthracite. In 1808 he succeeded with an L-shaped grate with spaced iron bars which, when installed in his tavern's fireplace, allowed a natural draft to sustain the fire.

In 1807 a local pioneer miner, Abijah Smith of Plymouth, hauled coal on an ark down the Susquehanna but was unsuccessful in its sale. Following Fell's success, Smith, now joined by his brother John, began a series of boat shipments to downriver markets. The brothers hired stone masons to accompany their coal shipment. When the masons demonstrated how the new grate worked the Smiths' coal found a ready market. The Smiths continued river shipments until the early 1820's.

Anthracite was also plentiful in the Schuylkill and Lehigh regions. The Schuylkill coal beds were discovered about 1790, and an early attempt by William Morris to sell a wagonload of coal in Philadelphia failed in 1800. In early 1812 George Shoemaker of Pottsville had nine wagons of coal shipped to Philadelphia for public sale. Apparently anthracite's poor reputation preceeded its arrival, since the hapless merchant could sell only two wagonloads. Forced to give away his remaining supply, Shoemaker was subjected to an angry mob who were unable to burn it in their fireplaces.

Besides being hard to ignite it was claimed that hard coal caused everything from death to baldness. On a more realistic level, the mountainous terrain of the anthracite fields made transporting coal a costly proposition, so that its expense as well as its obvious firing problems curbed its usage.

Coal was found near Mauch Chunk (now Jim Thorpe) in the Lehigh field in 1791. The following year the Lehigh Coal Mine Company was formed to ship coal on the Lehigh River to Philadelphia. This company failed, as did others.

Early forms of coal transportation included first canal boats and, later, railroads. Early rail systems were built to get the coal over the mountains to the canals.

The major market for coal from Wyoming Valley would ordinarily have been Philadelphia. But the merchants of Philadelphia, the early nation's premier seaport, found it cheaper to import soft coal from England or from Virginia than to haul it over the mountains from northeastern Pennsylvania.

Opportunity came when the War of 1812 closed off ports for the import of British and Virginia coal. In 1813-1814 there was an effort by Jacob Cist, Charles Miner, and John Robinson, representing Wyoming Valley investors, to reopen the Lehigh mines for shipping coal to Philadelphia. But with the war's end, this effort was curtailed, and English and Virginia coal again dominated the Philadelphia market.

Eventually, the development of a privately built canal system along the Schuylkill River in 1816-1825, followed by the construction of the Philadelphia and Reading Railroad in 1842, provided a lucrative transportation line to Philadelphia for Schuylkill coal. In 1818-1820 in the Lehigh region, the privately built Lehigh Coal and Navigation Company developed river transportation and gravity railroad systems to reach the eastern markets. Major canal improvements followed a few years later.

In the Wyoming field the North Branch Canal, with its Wyoming Division through the Wyoming Valley, was built along the Susquehanna River from Northumberland to Pittston between 1828 and 1834, part of a publicly funded statewide canal system. By 1829 the Delaware and Hudson Canal Company was drawing coal from the Carbondale area over inclined planes, and a canal system was in place which reached from Honesdale to the Hudson River and the New York market.

The canal system through Wyoming Valley stimulated the rapid development of the area's coal industry. The Schuylkill coal industry dominated the state coal market from 1828 to the end of the Civil War. The Wyoming and Lehigh regions produced roughly the same percentages of coal from the 1840's through the mid-1850's, after which Wyoming's coal sales surpassed the Lehigh's, but not the Schuylkill's. Then, after the Civil War, the Wyoming coal field's production began to outpace both of the other fields. By 1875 the Wyoming region was producing over fifty percent of the state's coal shipments. It maintained its production supremacy through the end of the coal era.

The area's dominance in coal was partly attributable to geologic features which made its coal cheaper to produce. With the construction of the canals, Wyoming Valley successfully overcame both its late entry into the Philadelphia market and its greater distance from the coastal ports. With the development of its rail systems, the county's mines were in easy reach of the New York and Great Lakes markets as well.

Abijah Smith's original coal prospecting site of 1807.

Abijah Smith's expanded coal operation in Plymouth.

Charles Miner, 1780-1865, wrote the 1845 History of Wyoming *after many years in the newspaper business and two terms as a representative to the U.S. Congress from southeastern Pennsylvania.*

Weighing cargoes of coal on the Lehigh Canal.

TRANSPORTATION SYSTEMS IN LUZERNE COUNTY

A view down the Susquehanna River showing early steamboat transportation.

West Pittston/Exeter Railroad Company engine.

Railroad companies helping in the clean up effort following the 1902 flood.

Transportation systems have played a major role in the development of Luzerne County. From the trails blazed by Native Americans to the highways and air routes of the modern era, residents of the region have depended upon the available transportation systems for their economic wellbeing.

The Native Americans established a number of paths that traversed the region that became Luzerne County. These included the Lackawanna Path, which connected present-day Pittston to Windsor, New York; the Lehigh Path, from Wilkes-Barre to Bethlehem; the Wyoming Path, from Sunbury to Wilkes-Barre; and the Nanticoke Path, from Calvert, Maryland, to Nanticoke. The trails were used for trade, hunting, seasonal visits to the seashore, and war. Many of these paths' routes eventually became highways.

The colonial settlers at first traveled on crude wagon trails. In 1772 a highway tax was imposed for improving the main routes. The present-day Pennsylvania Routes 115 and 92 were hacked out by the American army during Sullivan's March. In the early 1800's a number of turnpikes were constructed, connecting the county with key points in several directions.

The Susquehanna River was used as a trade and transportation route, but its lack of depth and rocky bottom made it inefficient. This prompted the construction of canals for transporting anthracite. Ground was first broken in 1828 for the North Branch Canal and, by 1834, the waterway extended from Shamokin Dam to Nanticoke with an extension connecting to Pittston, and by 1856 to Pennsylvania's northern tier. The trip from Shamokin Dam to Nanticoke took approximately fourteen and one-half hours and the barges could haul 260 tons of goods. However, by the time the canals were constructed to their furthest connecting points they were already being replaced by the railroads.

Railroads had the greatest cumulative impact upon Luzerne County's economic structure. The

Lehigh and Susquehanna Railroad was completed in 1846. It connected the valley's coal fields with White Haven and the transportation systems to the southeast, while the Lackawanna and Wyoming Valley Railroad and the Lackawanna and Bloomsburg Railroad shipped coal to the iron furnaces in Bloomsburg, Danville, and Sunbury.

Construction of Interstate 81 at Lake Nuangola looking north toward Wilkes-Barre.

The Lehigh Valley Railroad, first established in the Hazleton area coal fields, was connected to Wilkes-Barre in 1867. Two years later it linked Wilkes-Barre to Waverly, New York. The Lehigh Valley was not only an important transportation system but was also a powerful influence in the mining industry through its purchase of extensive coal lands in both the Hazleton and Wyoming Valley areas.

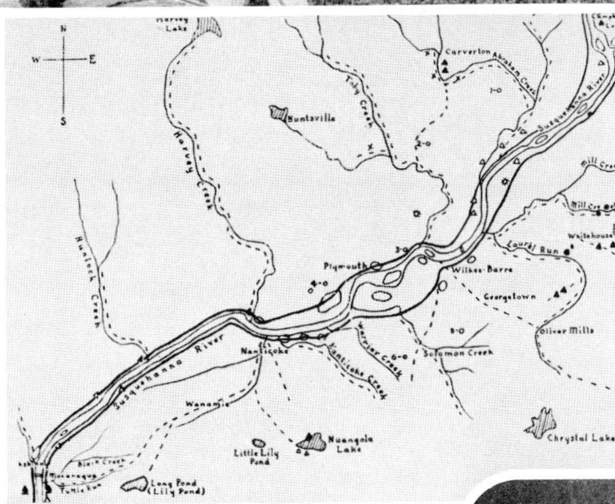

Map of Native American trails and settlements in the Wyoming Valley drawn by Max Schrabisch in 1926.

The decline of rail freight transportation in Luzerne County coincided with the demise of anthracite as a major economic force. Highways and air routes have been the dominant modes of transportation in the post-World War II period. The development of practical highway transportation dates back to the 1920's when Governor Gifford Pinchot instituted a program of extensive, low-cost highway construction. Pinchot's roads crisscrossed Luzerne County, allowing farmers to get their goods to the urban centers. The county was linked to other regions of the state and nation by a number of U.S. and Pennsylvania routes. U.S. 11 paralleled the Susquehanna River in Luzerne County on its course from Maine to Louisiana. Pennsylvania Route 309 was once the major route to Philadelphia while Route 115 linked the area to roads leading to New York. However, since these roadways ran through cities and towns, they were inefficient and time consuming for travelers.

The construction of limited access highways—the Northeast Extension of the Pennsylvania Turnpike in 1957 and Interstates 80 and 81 in the 1960's—brought a level of road transportation to the area that ensured the county's economic wellbeing. Today these roadways connect Luzerne County with major markets in all directions, and the intersection of Routes 80 and 81 in Butler Township has earned the appellation "Crossroads of America."

Portrait of Gifford Pinchot, Governor of Pennsylvania and later Chairman of the National Conservation Commission.

Luzerne County is linked to the nation and world by air transportation through the Wilkes-Barre/Scranton International Airport in Avoca. Operated jointly by the County Commissioners of Luzerne and Lackawanna counties, the airport opened in 1947. It undertook expansions in 1958 and 1962, and in 1975 was designated a port of entry by the United States Customs Service.

Luzerne County's changing economic structure is reflected in the development of its transportation systems. They served as an impetus to its early settlement, played a major part in the anthracite era, and were a key to the county's economic recovery in recent years.

Wilkes-Barre/Scranton International Airport at Avoca.

Mathias Hollenback, 1752-1829, came to Wyoming as one of the Paxtang Boys from Hanover, Pa., became a trader c. 1773, and began acquiring land. At the time of his death Judge Hollenback was probably the wealthiest man in northeastern Pennsylvania.

In the last third of the nineteenth century, the railroad corporations consolidated mining interests under their corporate umbrellas and dominated the economic fabric of the coal fields.

However, Wyoming Valley's capitalists had also built interlocking corporate controls into a far-reaching network of wealth and influence. Pooling their capital, they successfully prevented the complete takeover of the area's anthracite industry by capitalists from New York and Philadelphia.

Valley families such as the Hollenbacks, Butlers, Denisons, Nesbitts, Stewarts, and Conynghams became involved in a wide variety of enterprises related to mining. They dealt in buying, selling, and leasing land rights, shipping coal, and financing the institutions that supported the industry. Several of these entrepreneurs were descended from the early settlers and already owned large acreages in Wyoming Valley. They were able to acquire much more land, and in order to protect their ownership of the coal, sold surface properties separately from mineral rights, allowing coal to be mined under most of the valley.

Nineteenth century wealth in Luzerne County, as in America as a whole, was in the hands of a concentrated few who interacted in the same social circle. Many of the men attended Yale and other Ivy League colleges, while those interested in the operational aspects of the coal industry went to engineering schools such as Lafayette and Lehigh. They socialized at the Westmoreland Club, where they also transacted business deals, and tended to be clannish. Marriages often occurred between their families. Almost all were Presbyterian or Episcopalian, usually attending either First Presbyterian or St. Stephen's Episcopal Church in downtown Wilkes-Barre. Eventually they formed over twenty-five corporations, held thirty chief executive positions, and occupied one hundred board seats. By 1880 they had created a network of wealth and power in a single industry area where 92.2% of the employment was concentrated in the anthracite mines and related industries.

Since Wilkes-Barre's wealthy capitalists were one of the most potent economic forces in the area's anthracite fields, it is understandable that they had a tremendous impact upon the history of Luzerne County. As has been pointed out by Edward J. Davies in *The Anthracite Aristocracy*, and by Donald L. Miller and Richard E. Sharpless in *The Kingdom of Coal*, they were a major force in the lives of nearly 500,000 people. Living in a world of grace and comfort, they were separated

The Coal Exchange Building. Built in 1890, it contained the first passenger elevator in Wilkes-Barre.

Engineers in the Pardee & Co. drafting room.

Sheldon Reynolds, 1844-1895, lawyer and local historian.

First Presbyterian Church, Wilkes-Barre.

Left: St. Stephen's Episcopal Church of Wilkes-Barre, formally organized in 1821, has occupied the same site since 1822. The current structure was built in 1912.

Far Left: First Methodist Episcopal Church of Wilkes-Barre, organized in 1830, has been at the same location on North Franklin Street since 1849.

Abram Nesbitt, 1831-1920, entrepreneur and community benefactor, founded Nesbitt Hospital in Kingston in 1912.

from the hardships, poverty, and death associated with the mining industry, while the whole county, and the anthracite region in particular, depended upon them for their livelihoods.

On the other hand, this same small circle was responsible for bringing culture and community development to Wyoming Valley. They made Wilkes-Barre the wealthiest city in the anthracite region, which allowed other residents to achieve social mobility, and long after the era of anthracite ended, the institutions they founded continued to serve the county's residents. Nesbitt Hospital in Kingston and MMI Preparatory School in Freeland are two examples of this community legacy. Whether seen as solid American entrepreneurs, evil robber barons, or some combination of both, this nineteenth century elite affected the lives of most Luzerne County residents for nearly a century.

While Wilkes-Barre provided the capital and business acumen, the coal towns supplied the labor and services necessary for the huge anthracite industry. Two types of coal towns developed in Luzerne County—free towns and company towns. Free towns were usually those founded before the coal boom came. They were most numerous in Wyoming Valley. Here communities such as Kingston, Nanticoke, Pittston, and Plymouth were already well established, due to the valley's early growth along an artery of

Nesbitt Hall, gift of Abram Nesbitt to Wyoming Seminary, Kingston, in 1893.

Mine patch housing in Plymouth.

View of the Kingston Coal Company Colliery showing the tight integration of housing, railroad, and mining operations.

transportation located near good farmland. Towns such as these had already developed basic social, economic, and political systems. When coal was discovered it completely changed the lifestyle and ethnic complexion of these towns, but while the mine companies wielded considerable power there, they were never in total control.

Company towns, often referred to as "mine patches," came into existence as a direct result of the coal boom. Often found in the more rugged highlands of the Hazleton area and between established towns in Wyoming Valley, the location of these communities was based on their proximity to mine shafts and breakers. They were created by the mine companies for the sole purpose of providing housing for the workers.

Quoting from the *Hazleton Plain Speaker*, historian Harold W. Aurand has noted that "Everything in the region belongs to the operators and must be subject to their autocratic domination. They are the lords of the domain and no man is allowed to encroach on their territory..." In fact, these towns resembled feudal fiefs. The mine companies owned the homes and profited from the rent paid by the workers. They ran the overpriced company stores and often forced the miners to buy exclusively from them. Taverns, often the meeting places of miners in free towns, were usually banned in the company towns. The company was the law, and might omit such details as due process when dealing with their tenants. Scattered throughout the highlands of lower Luzerne County are villages such as Jeddo, Lattimer, and Pardeesville, which still show the remnants of their mine patch days.

Life in either type of town was often one of hardship. Homes were crowded together, both to minimize the distances required to walk to work, and to provide as much housing in a small space as possible. Community sanitation was almost non-existent. Outdoor toilets and open sewers were the common method of waste removal. Men often began their workday before sunrise and did not return home until after dark. Women, lacking any household conveniences and caring for very large families, toiled for even longer hours at home. With no workers' compensation and little insurance, the death or disability of the family breadwinner could mean destitution.

Tragedy was no stranger to the mining towns. Deaths occurred most often in accidents that affected one or two miners. However major disasters, such as that at Avondale in 1869, were also a fact of life. And mine workers who survived uninjured were often afflicted with anthracosilicosis, known as black lung disease, which robbed them of their ability to breathe normally.

Despite the difficulties of life in the coal towns, a spirit of camaraderie developed among the people sharing these harsh conditions, and many workers were earning the highest wages they had ever received. They built their lives around ethnic, and later, community institutions. Whether church, civic organization, or neighborhood tavern, these institutions eased the difficulties of life in the coal region.

Large scale mining operations brought marked change to the ethnic composition of Luzerne County. The region, at one time able to sustain only scattered farms and a few

DANGER IN THE MINES

"The coal mine calamity at Avondale, bringing the dead from the mine," from an 1869 issue of Frank Leslie's Illustrated Newspaper.

Coal miners and laborers always lived with the specter of death nearby. On average, ten miners were killed every week in the anthracite mines, and between the years 1894 and 1904, there were 5,001 deaths. Luzerne County suffered its share of these tragedies, including some major disasters.

The worst disaster took place in 1869 at Avondale, located two miles south of Plymouth. A fire was normally kept burning at the bottom of the shaft in order to force air circulation. During a late summer strike in 1869 the fire went out. On September 6 work resumed, but when the fire was re-ignited, flames raged out of control, igniting timbers, spreading up the ventilator shaft to the engine room, and destroying any means of transporting the workers from the mine below. The Avondale mine had only one opening and the trapped workers could not get any oxygen. For two days rescuers attempted to extinguish the fire and eliminate the deadly gases. All efforts were in vain, and when the rescue party did get into the mine they found the bodies of 108 men and boys. Many fathers and sons were holding each other, while others were pressing their faces against the dirt in the hope of getting some oxygen through it. Two rescue workers were overcome by mine gases, bringing the final death toll to 110.

Lithograph of the dark days of the scourge at Plymouth showing an early morning scene in the miners house and the arrival of the relief party.

An inaccurate mine map caused the death of seventeen men in Jeansville, south of Hazleton. Two miners set off a blast in an area that was supposedly sixty feet from an abandoned, flooded slope. Actually they were only five feet away and a torrent of water poured through into the mine. While the two miners who ignited the blast swam to safety, seventeen others were drowned. Miraculously, five workers were rescued after twenty-five days. They had stayed alive by eating their clothing and tree bark from the support timbers.

Nanticoke was the scene of two major disasters. In 1885 a miner dug into an area of mine residue that turned into quicksand. Twenty-six workers were killed when the muck broke through. Their bodies were never recovered. In 1904 ten men were killed at the Auchincloss colliery when an engineer lost control of the engine lowering a carriage down a mine shaft. It struck the platform below with such force that the bottom dropped out and the men fell 450 feet into 200 feet of water and drowned.

"Nanticoke mine calamity" as portrayed in Frank Leslie's Illustrated Newspaper *in Jan. 1886.*

The second most deadly disaster in the anthracite fields occurred at the Twin Shaft mine in Pittston Junction. On June 28, 1896, a large crew of workers was attempting to prevent a cave-in when the timbers supporting the mine collapsed. Fifty-eight men were entombed in the mine. Despite weeks of highly risky efforts to reach them, their bodies were never recovered.

Increased safety regulations and better training reduced the scope of the disasters by the mid-1900s, but mining continued to be dangerous work. On January 15, 1947, mine gas ignited at the Nottingham mine in Plymouth, and fifteen workers lost their lives. The last of the major disasters occurred in Port Griffith, near Pittston, on January 22, 1959. The Susquehanna River broke through the Knox Coal Company mine killing twelve workers and causing underground flooding throughout Wyoming Valley. As detailed in Chapter Five, this event effectively ended most underground mining in Luzerne County.

Each disaster brought pressure for increased safety measures. Following the Avondale disaster, for example, mines were required to have more than one exit. Unfortunately, tragedy always seemed the necessary first step toward stricter safety regulation.

Knox Mine Disaster, when a hole in the slope section of the mine under the Susquehanna River in Port Griffith caused underground flooding.

A group of breaker boys outside the Lehigh Valley Coal Company's Exeter colliery.

"Miners Pay Day" an illustration from Harper's Weekly, *Feb. 22, 1873.*

small towns, became part of America's Industrial Revolution. Employment opportunities for both skilled and unskilled mine laborers, along with jobs for industrial support workers, were available in the coal towns. While this attracted some migration from the outlying farm areas, the bulk of the new arrivals in the coal fields came from abroad. In this early period of industrialization thousands of immigrants from Wales, England, Ireland, and Germany traveled to Luzerne County. Although their numbers seem small compared to the massive post-1880 migration, they created a major change in the social and cultural, as well as economic, composition of Luzerne County.

Early breaker construction made way for improved technology with the engineering and architectural advancements of the 1930s. Here the Maxwell Breaker of the 1890s is dismantled during the construction of the Huber Breaker in 1937-1939. Glen Alden Coal Co., Ashley.

Will Roberts and Ben Davis inside the Nottingham mine shaft.

One of the difficulties in extracting coal in Luzerne County, or anywhere else in the United States during the first half of the nineteenth century, was the lack of skilled miners. Since the Industrial Revolution began in Great Britain a half century before it did in the United States, by the early 1800's coal mining there had attained the status of a skilled craft. South Wales and southwestern England were the centers of the British coal industry and by the 1820's, these areas had an abundance of miners and a shortage of work.

The promise of basic employment rather than any hope of higher wages and better working conditions attracted Welsh and English miners to America. Not all Welsh and English immigrant workers in the coal fields were skilled miners. Many toiled as unskilled laborers as well, but prior experience in Welsh and English mines meant that a higher percentage of the Welsh and English held skilled positions than did members of other ethnic groups.

By 1900 there were 21,552 Welsh immigrants and their offspring living in Luzerne County. Another 19,348 resided in Lackawanna County, a part of Luzerne County until 1878. In fact, about eleven percent of the Welsh immigrants to America settled in Luzerne County, with especially large numbers in Wyoming Valley and in the Hazleton area. Plymouth, Nanticoke, Pittston, Parsons (later part of Wilkes-Barre), and the Heights section of Wilkes-Barre all had influential Welsh communities.

The Welsh brought strong beliefs about religion and morality, and established at least fifty-four churches in the county, most often Congregationalist, Presbyterian (known at first as Calvinist Methodist), and Baptist. They placed great emphasis on a family-centered life and abstinence from alcoholic beverages. Their antiliquor attitude led the Welsh to condemn the Irish and later immigrant groups whose cultural attitude toward alcohol differed. This, combined with their higher positions in the mines, laid the groundwork for ethnic conflict.

Luzerne County's Welsh population had a tremendous impact upon education in the region. Family sacrifice combined with their somewhat better paid positions allowed the Welsh to keep their children in school longer. As the second and third generations obtained normal school and college degrees, they began to play a leading role in teaching and administering the region's school systems. In Plymouth and Kingston, in particular, those of Welsh ancestry held positions ranging from teachers in the elementary schools to directors on the school boards.

Although many of the original settlers in Luzerne County were of English stock, they had long since separated themselves from the British Isles. When new English immigrants came to work in the coal fields they formed their own ethnic communities in the coal towns of Wyoming Valley and the mine patches in and around Hazleton. While some joined the already established Episcopal and Methodist churches, others opted for establishing their own Primitive Methodist churches. This working class religion was transported mainly to the anthracite regions of Pennsylvania and in effect became an English ethnic church.

These skilled workers, like the Welsh, brought with them a long history of conflict with the Irish which was readily transplanted to their new home. Like the Welsh, they placed great importance on the success of their offspring, and as a result many of their children experienced a good deal of social and economic mobility. It is easy to forget that these English were also an immigrant group, but their adherence to their heritage is demonstrated by the fact that twelve Primitive Methodist churches still exist in Luzerne County today.

Welsh and English immigrants were able to establish their own ethnic identity, but they also had an easier time assimilating into American society than many other cultural groups. They were already familiar with many of the British traditions that had become a part of America's heritage. Almost all of them were members of a Protestant denomination that had a similar branch well-established in the United States, and since America was still overwhelmingly Protestant in the pre-Civil War era, the Welsh and English religious beliefs were an advantage.

The greatest advantage of both the English and Welsh was their language. All of the English and many of the Welsh immigrants

Lehigh & Wilkes-Barre Coal Company inspectors inside a coal breaker in Plymouth.

Above left: First Presbyterian Church of Hazleton, built in 1869.

Above: First Baptist Church. Built in 1848, it had the first town clock in Wilkes-Barre.

Left: Children at the Nottingham School in Plymouth.

First Welsh Presbyterian Church, South Meade and Northampton Streets, Wilkes-Barre, founded 1864.

spoke English. Although a large contingent of Welsh preferred to use their native language, many were bilingual. Others of Welsh ancestry, especially the second generation, opted for English. In many towns English speaking separatist congregations split off from the original Welsh churches, which in turn prompted the older churches to offer services in both languages. Thus the use of English became increasingly common in the Welsh community.

The general lifestyle of the Welsh and English immigrants also contributed to their greater acceptance. Since many held skilled positions in the mines and a high percentage were "teetotalers," Americans born in the county viewed them as a solid addition to productive middle-class society. As such, Luzerne County's establishment believed that the Welsh and the English immigrants would soon become, in the expression of the time, "real Americans."

The Irish were the largest group to arrive in Luzerne County prior to the Civil War. By 1870 approximately ten percent of the county residents were Irish immigrants. They began migrating to the region in the 1820's to work on the construction of the North Branch Canal. Although many left again for work opportunities in Philadelphia, New York, or the lower anthracite fields, some remained in Wyoming Valley.

The great migration of Irish to Luzerne County came during the 1840's when the three year loss of the potato crop caused widespread starvation. The Potato Famine forced whole villages to emigrate to America, Canada, Australia, and New Zealand. Since most of the Irish were farmers and had neither skilled trades nor enough money to purchase land, they had little choice but to find unskilled work. The migration to the United States coincided with the growth of the coal industry in Luzerne County where there was a great need for unskilled workers in the mines and the collieries.

By the 1840's, Irish Americans had already established ethnic enclaves in Wilkes-Barre, Pittston, and Hazleton. Like other immigrant groups they centered their communities around their churches. In 1842, Irish Americans in Wilkes-Barre founded St. Mary's of the Immaculate Conception, the first Roman Catholic parish in Luzerne County, soon followed by new churches in Pittston and Hazleton. Although the Irish settled first in these older communities, many also made their homes in the small coal towns and villages in the region.

Scattered throughout the county, it was more difficult for the Irish-Americans in Luzerne County to establish the large cohesive ethnic communities that their counterparts

Irish immigrants John P. and Anna (Hannon) Kelly and their children. Parsons, c. 1918.

created in New York and Philadelphia. As a result they took longer to forge the same kind of political and societal power achieved more rapidly in the tight-knit urban centers.

Poverty and discrimination were a fact of life for the Irish immigrants in Luzerne County. Because most workers were not skilled, their pay was only two or three dollars per week compared to the eight dollars that a Welsh or English miner could make. In lower Luzerne County many lived in company towns, and the bulk of their paychecks went right back into the hands of the mine operators in the form of rent and bills from the company store. They were often the last hired, and in bad times, the first fired. Work was sporadic. If a laborer was called out to work 250 days during the year he was lucky. It was often necessary for the children to work in order for the family to meet their basic needs. The daughters of the laborers found work as housekeepers for the more affluent families, while the sons toiled as breaker boys in the collieries. Although twelve was the usual age for entering the labor force, it was not unusual to see younger children working.

Irish Americans faced a great deal of discrimination. Roman Catholicism was long mistrusted by British Protestants in the Old World and they brought their prejudices to America. There was a fear harking back to Queen Mary Tudor's time that Catholics were intent on conquest, and that the Irish immigrants were some sort of advance force sent by the Pope. On the other hand, the Irish had not forgotten Oliver Cromwell's conquest of Ireland. To compound this conflict of many generations, the temperance movement was growing, and its adherents were pushing for the prohibition of alcoholic beverages. A great deal of ethnic tension resulted.

The problems of geographic separation, poverty, and discrimination common to all Irish Americans in the anthracite region were compounded for those in Luzerne County. In Carbon and Schuylkill Counties some Irish were able to strike out against unfair labor conditions by means of the legendary Molly Maguires. In these counties and in the Scranton area the Ancient Order of Hibernians helped unify

The first Catholic parish in Wilkes-Barre was established in 1842. St. Mary's of the Immaculate Conception Roman Catholic church has occupied its present site on South Washington Street since 1849.

Plymouth Coal Company breaker boys.

A meeting of the Molly Maguires as shown by an artist for Harper's Weekly *in 1874.*

the Irish community. In Scranton the Irish established a formidable elite. But in Luzerne County the grip of the establishment, buttressed by the Welsh and English, was so strong that it prevented the Irish from gaining political or economic power until well into the 1900s.

German Americans were an equally important ethnic group in nineteenth century Luzerne County. Many Pennsylvania Germans had farmed the valleys and hillsides of southern Luzerne County since colonial times. Although still adhering to some traditions, most had become Americanized by the 1840s. About that time the industrial growth in Luzerne County began to attract Germans directly from Europe. Skilled miners, however, did not emigrate. Miners in Germany, unlike those in Great Britain, had a strong labor organization and benefits regulated by the state.

Some of these later German immigrants also became farmers, but many farmers from the German states became laborers in the mines, and many more settled in towns compared to their seventeenth and eighteenth century predecessors. Wilkes-Barre and Hazleton both had large German communities, which included skilled craftsmen who found work in the building trades and industrial support businesses, as well as mine laborers. In fact, skilled German bricklayers were responsible for some of Wilkes-Barre's most beautiful nineteenth century structures, such as the Stegmaier Brewery. Because of this sizeable population, German Americans in the county published over ten German language newspapers at various times, including the *Wachter*, which was in circulation for ninety years.

The German ethnic experience was more diverse than that of some other national groups. Among the German immigrants were major differences in geographic, religious,

Left: Mt. Zion Church, built in 1892, housed both Lutheran and Reformed congregations in Slocum Township.

Below: Zion Evangelical Church, Hazleton

Bottom: The German Reformed Church at South Main and South Streets, Wilkes-Barre, was built in 1850. Purchased by St. Paul's Lutheran congregation, it is now the Good Shepherd Lutheran Church, the oldest standing church structure in the city.

and economic backgrounds. But like most other immigrant groups there was a tendency to organize chiefly along religious lines. Between 1837 and 1880, eight houses of worship were established in Wilkes-Barre alone, including Lutheran, Reformed, Evangelical United Brethren, Roman Catholic, and Reformed Jewish congregations, although some of the Protestants who migrated to the area affiliated with already established German Protestant churches. The German Catholics and Jews faced the same religious prejudices as the Irish, derived largely from attitudes imported directly from Europe.

The German Jews brought significant business and commercial experience with them, acquired in Europe where they were seldom allowed to own land. Combined with an ethnic culture that believed in hard work, they were able to establish themselves in a variety of much needed businesses in the county. Transferring these business skills to America they sometimes achieved social and economic stability relatively quickly, which aggravated any bias against them.

Despite their problems, most German families were able to move up the social and economic ladder. Such factors as skilled crafts, prior commercial experience, and in the case of the Protestants, similar religious practices, helped them overcome the language and culture barriers to succeed in Luzerne County.

Life in the region increasingly centered around the coal towns, but thousands of people still relied on farming for their livelihoods. It was not an easy life, requiring a great deal of hard work and skill to obtain any bounty from the soil. In fact, by mid-century, much of the county's best farm-

The B'nai B'rith congregation was incorporated in 1848 and dedicated this first synagogue on South Washington Street, Wilkes-Barre, in August, 1849.

land was lost, having been located in areas that were being mined.

The mountains and rough roads isolated those living in the outlying areas, and the coal towns drew young people away from the farms. As mentioned earlier, the majority of the farmers in northern Luzerne County were Methodists and Baptists of Connecticut descent. From Mountaintop southward people of predominately Lutheran and Reformed German background, who had migrated to the area from both southern Pennsylvania and the German states, tilled the soil.

The coal boom made agriculture secondary to industry in the county, but there was one advantage to increasing urbanism. Farmers had a ready market for their goods. The landscape, soil, and climate were well suited to dairy farming, and local farmers could find outlets for their milk products both locally and in other eastern cities. As a result, by the end of the nineteenth century dairy farming was the leading agricultural business in Luzerne County.

The Civil War had a major effect on the lives of Luzerne County's inhabitants during this period. Residents fought in 27 different regiments and saw action in most of the major campaigns. On Luzerne County's perimeter, in Columbia, Schuylkill, Sullivan, and Wyoming counties, pockets of anti-war sentiment existed. In the rural areas of Columbia, Sullivan, and Wyoming counties, the more isolated farmers believed they had no real stake in the outcome of the conflict. In Schuylkill County many Irish mine workers feared that emancipation of the slaves would increase the competition for low-paying unskilled labor. Although Luzerne County had large numbers of both Irish laborers and isolated farmers, there was less outright opposition to the war effort. Most municipalities

The Honorable George W. Woodward served as a Pennsylvania Supreme Court justice from 1853 to 1864 and then as Chief Justice until 1868. Although he lost the gubernatorial race in 1863, he was elected to the U.S. Congress in 1867 and 1868.

fulfilled their enlistment obligations, and a strong sense of patriotism prevailed.

Some prominent citizens, however, were not behind President Abraham Lincoln's war efforts. Pennsylvania State Supreme Court Justice George W. Woodward, a Wilkes-Barre native, was the unsuccessful Democratic candidate for governor in 1863. An advocate for Pennsylvania's secession from the Union, Woodward was identified with the Peace Democrats, who sought to reach an accord with the Confederacy.

In Luzerne County, despite the formation of Wyoming, Susquehanna, Bradford, and Lackawanna counties from its original territory, the population grew from 18,109 in 1810 to nearly 150,000 in 1880. Wilkes-Barre was incorporated as a city on May 4, 1871, while Hazleton grew from a country crossroads into a thriving coal town. Wealth, job opportunities, and booming communities existed side by side with poverty, dangerous working conditions, and ethnic antagonisms. Economic and social diversity made unity difficult, but upward mobility eased poverty for many, and the process of Americanization helped reduce ethnic tension. The period from 1880 to 1920 witnessed even greater industrial expansion and more dramatic change in the county, multiplying both the problems and rewards.

Dallas United Methodist Church.

LIFE ON THE FARM IN THE 1800s

Life on Luzerne County's farms was family-centered. Like agrarian cultures worldwide, large families were an economic asset, and ten or more children were not uncommon. Farm families lived on scattered plots of land separated from their neighbors by tracts of woodland, in log cabins supplanted by the mid-1800s with wood frame houses. Although mechanization was making inroads into the county by the mid-nineteenth century, farmers still relied on horses and mules, and families with large herds continued to need many children to help with the time consuming task of milking cows by hand. By the 1820s, homespun had given way to storebought clothing and other goods.

The monotony and isolation of farmlife was interrupted by church events and community socials. Although whiskey was produced and consumed in the mountains from the time of earliest settlement, by the 1840's a growing movement toward temperence was evident in the farmlands as well as the urban areas of the county.

Despite the hardships of farm life, there was a certain satisfaction to be gained from this independent, self-sufficient lifestyle. However, the growing influence of the anthracite industry, the increased mechanization of farming, and the advent of large-scale commercial agriculture eventually brought an end to traditional farmlife in Luzerne County.

Lumber milling yard at #4 colliery, Kingston Coal Co., 1918.

Hazleton's Cranberry Breaker under construction, 1896.

A group of Civil War Veterans gather in Edwardsville to commemorate Decoration Day on Wyoming Avenue in 1880.

H.J. Wagner, meat wagon, Wilkes-Barre. c.1900.

CHAPTER THREE

New Cultures and Old Traditions

The years following the American Civil War witnessed the greatest industrial expansion in history. With the advent of more advanced technological and transportation systems, new markets were created. Consequently, countless new workers were needed to labor in the mines, mills and factories of America. Because of the increased degree of mechanization, these new workers did not need to be skilled craftsmen. Most of the jobs called for unskilled laborers to toil alongside the machines.

Coal stove and furnace designs from the Pittston Stove Company, which existed from 1820 to 1928.

Millions of immigrants from eastern and southern Europe came to the United States to take advantage of the abundant employment opportunities. Spurred on by poor economic conditions at home and the inception of less expensive steamship transportation, they began to trickle into the industrial centers of the northeast and the midwest during the 1870s. By the 1880s the migration was in full force. The phenomenon peaked around 1900 and was largely curtailed by 1915, with the onset of World War I and the growing movement toward immigration regulation in America. During this period over fifteen million new arrivals came to America. Approximately seventy percent remained here, and most settled in urban industrial areas.

Luzerne County again reflected the developments in America as a whole. With increased urbanization went a greater need for home heating fuel. Since the mines of northeastern Pennsylvania were the closest source to the eastern metropolitan centers, and anthracite was the cleanest and most efficient fuel, the demand for this hard coal increased dramatically. Mechanization in the coal industry lessened the demand for highly skilled miners and brought about an increased need for unskilled laborers. Along with this, service workers were needed to meet the consumer needs of the growing population. In addition, by

Women at work in the winding department of the Atwood Silk Mill, West Main Street, Plymouth.

the turn of the century, thousands of jobs became available for women in the textile and garment industries. Although exact numbers are difficult to determine, it is likely that over 100,000 immigrants found employment in the coal towns of Luzerne County.

Ethnic organizations often originated in churches. Shown here are (clockwise from top) Lithuanian, Russian and Ulrainian Choruses, 1924.

Who were these new arrivals? Although significant numbers of Welsh, English, Irish, Germans, and even some Scandinavians continued to find new homes in Luzerne County, the vast majority of these later immigrants came from eastern and southern Europe and were of peasant stock. Their ethnic and cultural background, in approximate order of their numbers, was Polish, Italian, Slovak, Lithuanian, Ukrainian, Jewish, Ruthenian, Hungarian, Lebanese, Syrian, Greek, Slovenian, Croation, Serbian, and Tyrolian. In his groundbreaking 1905 study, *Anthracite Coal Communities*, Peter Roberts stated that twenty-six languages were spoken throughout the coal regions. An examination of this statistic shows that all of these languages were used in Luzerne County, the most populous of the anthracite counties.

Glen Alden Coal Company sign gives notice in English, German, Hungarian, Italian, Slovene, Serbo-Croat, and Polish. c. 1890

Poles were the largest group of new immigrants to settle in Luzerne County. Although a few Poles did settle in Nanticoke before the Civil War, they did not begin to arrive in large numbers until the 1870s, when Poland was divided among the three European monarchies of Germany, Austria-Hungary, and Russia.

The first Poles in the area migrated from the German section of Poland, at that time a part of East Prussia. Most settled in Nanticoke, where, in 1874, they established St. Stanislaus' Roman Catholic Church, the first Polish parish in the county. Because of their earlier arrival, and because they often had slightly better financial resources and education than later arrivals from other parts of Poland, many of the Prussian Poles became ethnic leaders in the late 1880s.

Prussian Polish migration to Luzerne County peaked by the end of the 1880s. At this time an increasing number of migrants from the Austro-Hungarian and Russian Empires were making their homes in Luzerne County. Although Nanticoke continued to attract large numbers of Poles from all three nations, by 1900 Polish settlements could be found throughout Luzerne County. Besides Nanticoke, Hazleton, Wilkes-Barre, Plymouth, Glen Lyon, and Plains Township all had large enough Polish American communities to support more than one ethnic church. Other enclaves were found in Pittston, Hanover Township, Kingston, Larksville, Freeland, Wyoming, Exeter, and Mocanaqua.

Numerous Poles also became farmers in the rural regions of the county, especially in and around Dorrance, Lake Silkworth, and Fairmount Springs. Since the census and immigration records of that time listed country of origin but not ethnicity, it is difficult to ascertain the exact number of Polish immigrants to Luzerne County. The fact that many left the region for other American cities or to return to their Old World homes adds to the problem. However, it is estimated that there were at least 30,000 Polish immigrants in the county at any given time between 1890 and 1910. Combined with their American born descendants, that translates to at least fifteen to twenty percent of the county population having a Polish heritage.

The second largest of the new immigrant groups were the Italians. There were probably at least 14,000 Italian immigrants in the county during the period between 1890 to 1910. This migration started in the northern regions of the Italian peninsula in the 1870s, and shifted southward through the 1880s and 1890s. Because Italy did not become unified until 1870, many of the new arrivals to America retained their regional loyalties rather than seeing themselves as Italians. For example an immigrant might identify himself or herself as Sicilian or Perugian rather than Italian. At times, this localism caused some animosity between the different groups of Italian immigrants in Luzerne County.

The greatest concentrations of Italian Americans in the county were in the

The Polish Falcons Band at St. Stanislaus Church, 1918.

Charles Bebee residence, an early farm home in Dallas Township.

Norman Stairs' blacksmith shop, Dallas Township. c. 1900

The Italian Royal Band in front of the Hazle Township Municipal Building.

The Knights of Lithuania Baseball Team, Hazleton, 1930.

Hazleton and Pittston areas. A smaller settlement was located in the Heights section of Wilkes-Barre. In Hazleton alone the Italians founded three ethnic Roman Catholic churches, with additional ones nearby in Freeland and Lattimer. In the Pittston area, two Italian Catholic churches were established in Pittston and one in Exeter.

Lithuanians arriving in Luzerne County were often perceived as Polish. The former union of Poland and Lithuania, their arrival during the same period as the Poles, and their inclusion along with Polish parishioners in the early ethnic churches contributed to the misunderstanding. However, Lithuanians were a distinct ethnic and cultural group, and unlike most of the other eastern Europeans, they were not Slavic.

Lithuanians first began to arrive in the Plymouth, Hazleton, and Pittston areas in the 1880s. After a stormy relationship in a parish shared with Poles, the Lithuanians in the Plymouth area established their first church, St. Casmir's, in nearby Larksville. (It was later moved to Hanover Township.) Lithuanian communities were soon founded in

GREATER PITTSTON: HOME TO SUPERSTARS

During the past century these very outstanding athletes from the Pittston area gained renown in major sports. They began their careers in and around Pittston, and their successes carried them to the top in national competition.

Hughie Jennings attracted widespread attention in baseball just as the sport was becoming a national phenomenon in the late 1800s. During a career that lasted from 1891 to 1918 he is remembered as one of the best shortstops and contact hitters of the early game. Jennings led the Baltimore Orioles to three straight National League pennants and later managed the Detroit Tigers to an American League pennant. A lifetime .314 hitter, he was inducted into the Hall of Fame in 1945. Sadly, he never witnessed this honor, having died of meningitis in 1928.

Hughestown resident Bucky Harris became known as the "Boy Wonder" of baseball after he managed the Washington Senators to a 1924 World Series championship. He managed for 29 years in the Majors with the Detroit Tigers, Boston Red Sox, Philadelphia Phillies, and New York Yankees, in addition to the Senators. Harris captured another World Series with the Yankees. He retired in 1956 and was inducted into the Hall of Fame in 1975.

Charlie Trippi was a two-time All Scholastic for Pittston High School in 1938 and 1939. After a year at LaSalle Academy he went to the University of Georgia. In 1942 he played in the Rose Bowl against the University of California at Los Angeles. His college career was interrupted while he served in the Air Force during World War II. Upon his return to Georgia he participated in the Sugar Bowl in 1946 and was named All-American. He played professional football with the Chicago Cardinals and was named All-Pro in 1947 and 1948. In 1968 he was named to the professional football Hall of Fame in Canton, Ohio.

Jimmy Cefalo was one of the nation's most heavily recruited football players when he graduated from Pittston Area High School in 1974. He was Pennsylvania's leading ground gainer with 4,449 yards rushing. Cefalo pleased local fans by attending Penn State, where he starred as a wide receiver. In 1976, he was named Most Valuable Player in the Cotton Bowl. He continued his football career with the Miami Dolphins. After seven years in the National Football League, Cefalo began a new career in broadcast journalism. He appeared on the "Today" show and "NBC News at Sunrise," and received an Emmy Award for sports writing during the 1988 Seoul Olympic Games.

Duryea's Gene Guarilla starred in basketball for George Washington University and was the second-round draft choice for the Boston Celtics in 1959. He played on four National Basketball Association championship teams with the legendary Celtics. After his retirement Guarilla returned to the area and served as a teacher and coach at Pittston Area High School.

Pittston area residents can take great pride in the accomplishments of these athletes. Not only were their achievements outstanding, but they received top recognition from sports fans throughout America.

Kingston, Luzerne, Wilkes-Barre, Sugar Notch, Dorrance, the Hanover Section of Nanticoke, and Wanamie. The average Lithuanian population in Luzerne County in the late 1800s and early 1900s was approximately 9,000.

About 9,000 Slovak immigrants had also settled in Luzerne County by the turn of the century. They first settled in Nanticoke, and soon after communities could be found in Pittston, Hazleton, Freeland, Plymouth, Ashley, Kingston, Swoyersville, Larksville, and Mocanaqua. Three ethnic parishes were eventually formed in Wilkes-Barre, and the North End section of that city became a center for Slovak life and culture in the region. Here, the Reverend Joseph Murgas became not only a community leader, but was also responsible for important discoveries in the field of wireless communication.

Immigrants who followed the Eastern Rite practices of Catholicism constituted the fifth largest new immigrant group in the county. The adherents to Eastern Catholicism were from a variety of cultural and geographic backgrounds. Included in this group are Ukrainians, who probably numbered about 3,500, and Sub-Carpathian Rusyns (also referred to as Ruthenians), numbering about 2,000. Ukrainians migrated from western sections of the Russian Empire and the Galicia region of the Austro-Hungarian Empire. Ruthenians came mostly from the Hungarian region of Austria-Hungary. Because of this diversity it was difficult for Eastern Rite Catholics to form a cohesive group. The first Eastern Rite church in Luzerne County was founded in Kingston in 1887, and subsequent parishes were established in Hazleton, Freeland, Wilkes-Barre, Swoyersville, Glen Lyon, Nanticoke, Pittston, Plymouth, Edwardsville, Alden, and Georgetown. Eventually, dissension between the Ukrainians and the Ruthenians led to the creation of separate Eastern Rite churches. As will be shown later in the chapter, the differing practices of Eastern Rite Catholics and the dominant Roman Catholics resulted in serious confrontations between the two groups.

East European Jews were another important immigrant group in Luzerne County. Adherents to the Orthodox branch of the Jewish faith, they were often quite different in appearance and attitude from the Germanic Reformed Jews who had settled in the county a generation earlier. However, as with their German counterparts, restrictions on land ownership in Europe had often forced the Jews in the Russian and Austro-Hungarian Empires into small commercial and business ventures. Upon arrival in America, many served the coal towns as merchants and shopkeepers.

Since East European Jews came to America to avoid religious persecution rather than for economic advancement, they usually came as a complete family. This added

Born in Czecho-Slovakia, Rev. Joseph Murgas became pastor of Sacred Heart Roman Catholic Church in 1896. Among his many accomplishments he is credited with developing the first workable system of overland wireless telegraphy and radio.

Slovak wedding party, Swoyersville, 1928.

The Jewish Synagogue, Temple B'nai B'rith, Washington St., Wilkes-Barre, was dedicated in 1881, following the destruction of the original Temple B'nai B'rith which was dedicated in 1849.

An early Greek Catholic Church in Hazleton.

stability helped them to establish themselves more readily in Luzerne County. Jewish Orthodox communities could be found in most of the coal towns. In Wilkes-Barre's Heights section alone there were four Orthodox synagogues, and Pittston, Swoyersville, Nanticoke, Hazleton, Plymouth, Luzerne, Edwardsville, Exeter, and Miners Mills had one each. Altogether between 2,000 and 3,000 Orthodox Jews resided in Luzerne County around 1900.

Immigrants from the eastern Mediterranean were able to establish viable ethnic communities in Wilkes-Barre where about 800 Lebanese, 500 Syrians and 300 Greeks resided. They founded two Lebanese Maronite Rite churches, one Syrian Antiochian, and one Greek Orthodox. While some of these immigrants worked in the mines, a fairly high percentage of all three groups were merchants. They were especially successful in the food and produce businesses and as scrap metal dealers.

The McNeal Coal Company currency for the Yatesville Colliery stating "Storekeeper pay to bearer FIVE DOLLARS in Merchandise," 1872.

This massive influx of immigrants into America and Luzerne County created many myths. One of the most persistent and most inaccurate is that they came to America for religious and political freedom. While this may have been true of earlier immigrants, and was certainly true for many Jews, most of the new immigrants were faithful members of the established state churches in their homelands. In effect, they actually exposed themselves to more religious discrimination by coming to America.

As to political freedom, these immigrants had never before experienced democracy. Living by the rules in their homelands, however, they would most likely have avoided political persecution. The major political concern for most young men was the military draft. This prompted some reluctant soldiers to make the trip to America, but the numbers were not high.

The overwhelming reason for coming to Luzerne County was readily available employment. This may not seem as high-minded as political and religious freedom, nor as appealing as avoiding military service, but, as with most cases of migration to and within America, the chief reason for coming to Luzerne County was economic.

Although there was no single immigrant experience, a common pattern of settlement and development for these new arrivals could be observed. With the exception of the East European Jews, most of the first arrivals were young single men or married men whose wives remained in the old country. Their objective was to work in the mines for a few years and save enough money to return home financially secure. Actually, almost one-third of these men did go back to the old country. Others left Luzerne County after a few years to find more lucrative or steadier employment in the soft coal fields or in an industrial city. But most, despite their original intention to return home, eventually decided to remain in America.

Upon arrival in Luzerne County an immigrant would attempt to make a connection with someone of the

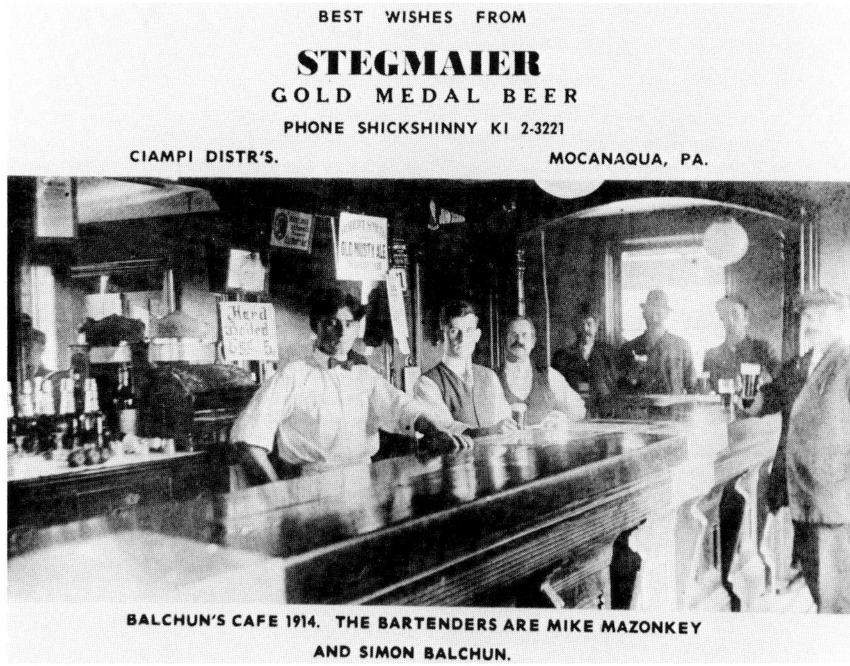

Advertisement for Stegmaier Gold Medal Beer showing Balchun's Cafe in Shickshinny in 1914.

same ethnic background who had some experience in the New World. For the young men who first came to the coal fields this meeting most likely would take place in a local tavern. Although the "beer garden" most certainly provided drink for miners "to wash the dust down" after a hard day's work, it also served a number of business functions. Here the new arrival could find someone who could direct him to a job and a place to live. The job would more than likely be employment as an underground or above ground unskilled laborer in the coal industry. The usual residence was a boarding house operated by the wife of one of the new arrival's fellow mine workers. For a reasonable rate the boarding house would provide lodging and meals. The lodging was usually relatively clean, although somewhat crowded, and the food was substantial.

After the initial influx of young men into the coal towns, women began to arrive in larger numbers. Some were the wives of the mine workers, who usually remained in their homelands until their husbands had secured steady employment, but many of the women who migrated were young and single. Some made the journey with family or friends, while others ventured to the New World alone and made contacts on arrival. Whether a woman's family was in America or remained in the old country, it was often necessary for these women to find employment in order to supplement the household income.

At first, many women worked as housekeepers in the homes of "the English," as the more established English-speaking residents were commonly known. However, by the turn of the century, textile and garment manufacturers recognized the abundance of female workers in the county. Consequently, over twenty large textile mills and countless garment factories of all sizes were established in Luzerne County. Although female employment was often interrupted by marriage and family, many women went back to work in the mills and factories on a part-time or full-time basis when their children were older. During the frequent slack times in the mines, their paychecks were not simply second incomes. The women were often, in fact, the principal wage earners.

There was, of course, a tendency for immigrants of similar ethnic backgrounds to settle near each other. In Luzerne County there was often "chain migration," or a pattern where immigrants of the same village or region in the old country would settle close to each other in the coal towns. For example, Poles from Galicia gravitated to the lower end of Plymouth. By doing this, an ethnic community was formed. All of the larger coal towns, such as Wilkes-Barre, Hazleton, Nanticoke, Kingston, Pittston, and Plymouth had a variety of different cultural enclaves. Even though a town may have gained the reputation for being Polish or Italian, there were actually many ethnic groups residing in each municipality. Nanticoke, while being widely regarded as a Polish community, never had more than half its population from that ethnic group. Pittston was considered an Italian town when less than one-third of its

Women in Luzerne County's Workforce

Female workers in Luzerne County have long been a central part of the region's economic life. When steady employment in the mines could not be counted on, wives and daughters often provided the most stable income. However, while the lives of the miners have been well documented the story of the women in Luzerne County's textile mills and cigar and garment factories has received less attention. The inclusion of such large numbers of women in the workforce had important social and economic effects upon the county.

Twin houses in Wilkes-Barre used as hospitals in the 1901 smallpox epidemic.

In the latter half of the nineteenth century, leaders in the textile and garment industry recognized the vast pool of female labor in the anthracite region. At first the mills and factories were interested in the unmarried daughters of the mine workers. However, when compulsory education became commonplace in the twentieth century, the wives of the miners were also recruited into the workforce. The fact that many of these women came from Slavic backgrounds, where it was acceptable for a married women to work outside of the home, made Luzerne County even more attractive to the textile and garment industry.

In 1920 slightly less than fifteen percent of the employed in Luzerne County were women. By 1950 that figure had risen to over thirty percent. Of these 42,137 women workers over three-fourths were in manufacturing or textiles. When mine workers averaged only two or three days of work per week, the women in the mills and factories could work a full schedule that often included the opportunity for overtime. Despite their efforts in the workplace, however, women generally averaged less than half the salary of men. The argument was often made that female employees were only supplementing the family income. Considering the fact that many women were the principal breadwinners in Luzerne County families, this argument lacked validity.

Predominantly female work force shown at the opening of the Neisner Brothers Store in Wilkes-Barre.

What impact did the presence of such a large female workforce have on Luzerne County? Despite the dire predictions of some, there were few negative effects upon Luzerne County's social and economic structure. First and foremost women workers kept many families from financial disaster, during both the labor strife of the 1920s and the decline of anthracite in the 1950s. While some male egos may have been bruised in the process, it has also been theorized that the financial input of women made them equal partners in household management and created a more gender-balanced family. Finally, there is little evidence to suggest that children suffered. Historian Caroline Golab has shown that the unemployed fathers or the extended families cared for the children while the mothers worked. In her studies of Polish American families, an ethnic group with a high percentage of working mothers, the children showed a relatively low incidence of juvenile delinquency and demonstrated a strong sense of family values.

The history of women workers in Luzerne County can serve as a guide to understanding the impact of the changing workforce in America's recent past. While this phenomenon has transformed America in the last three decades, it has been a fact of life in Luzerne County for over a century.

residents were of Italian heritage. Even in the sections of the coal towns where a certain immigrant group dominated, there was still a mix of people. Coal Street in Plymouth was the center of that town's Galician Polish community, but a look at the 1910 census reveals that English and Welsh immigrants, as well as inhabitants of several generations, made their homes there. But since the appearance of the immigrants was so unfamiliar to most older residents, it sometimes seemed as if the new arrivals dominated the town.

Parish Committee of the Resurrection of the Lord Polish National Catholic Church, Zerby Avenue, Edwardsville, 1928.

The establishment of an ethnic church was an important task for the new immigrants. Although the great majority were Roman Catholic, it has been noted that there were also large numbers of Byzantine Catholics, Eastern Orthodox, and Orthodox Jews. Many of the coal towns already had a Roman Catholic church founded by the Irish or Germans, but the Slavs and Italians resisted attending mass presided over by a "foreigner." Adherents to Eastern Rite Catholicism and Orthodox Judaism had no choice but to establish their own religious sites since none existed in the region. All told, the new immigrants founded over 115 churches and synagogues in Luzerne County.

Certain members of these new immigrant groups so strongly resisted Irish domination of the diocese that schisms occurred. The establishment of the Polish National Catholic Church is the most dramatic example of this. Father Francis Hodur left his pastorate in Nanticoke for St. Stanislaus, a Polish splinter parish in Scranton that had seceded from the Sacred Hearts Parish, bought its own property, and begun construction of its own church. This change did not have the authorization of Bishop William O'Hara, then very elderly, nor of his coadjutor, Bishop Michael Hoban. After failing to gain approval from the Pope, Father Hodur broke with the Roman Catholic Church. The PNC eventually spread throughout the United States and Canada with over 250,000 faithful. In Luzerne County alone they built seven churches.

Holy Resurrection Russian Orthodox Church, Middle Road, Alden Station.

The Eastern Catholics had no established churches in the New World at the time of the mass immigration. Adherents to this branch of Christianity had to form their own parishes. The practices of Eastern Catholicism, including married clergy, were more akin to Eastern Orthodoxy than to the Roman Rite, and problems occurred with the Roman Catholic bishops. Eventually the Eastern Catholics were allowed to establish their own dioceses. Many felt such animosity toward the Roman establishment, however, that they converted to the Russian Orthodox Church during the early 1900s. Between 1887 and 1924, six Orthodox churches were established by the Ukrainians and Ruthenians in Luzerne County.

A number of the immigrants from Northern Italy belonged to the reformed tradition, and on arrival they founded the Second Presbyterian Church of Pittston. The dissatisfaction of the Italian Catholics

St. Mary's Byzantine Catholic Church, Fern Street, Freeland, in 1907

Mine surveying crew at the slope mine entrance. Drifton Colliery, c. 1890.

with the Roman Catholic hierarchy, combined with the dissatisfaction of the Irish American bishops with what they considered an Italian tendency toward folk worship, led many of the Italians to convert to Protestantism after their arrival in the county. A number became Pentacostal Protestants, a branch of Christianity which did not discourage overt displays of faith. Although most Italians remained Catholic, the converted Italian Protestants established more churches in Wyoming Valley than the Italian Catholics did.

Life was not easy for new immigrants in Luzerne County. They faced discrimination from the established inhabitants who did not understand their culture. In an 1894 book, *The Wyoming Valley in the Nineteenth Century*, by S.R. Smith, it was stated, "When the "Boys in Blue" returned (from the Civil War) they found an enemy more malignant than the gentleman aristocrat of the South. This enemy was fresh from Europe." Although this reference was directed at the Irish, it demonstrates the strong bigotry often displayed toward the later immigrants as well.

Since the eastern and southern Europeans came to the region at a time when industrial expansion was responsible for increased urbanization, there was a strong tendency to blame them for the turmoil that accompanied the rapid growth of the coal towns. In reality, the new immigrants were the worst victims of such urban problems as poverty, crime, and alcoholism—not the cause. If blame is to be placed, it belonged to the uncontrolled expansion of the coal industry and the mining towns.

In addition to the ever-present dangers of working in the mines, the mine workers in Luzerne County faced unemployment and underemployment, low wages, and domination by large, impersonal corporations. By the end of the nineteenth century, most mine operations in Luzerne County were controlled by large conglomerates such as the railroads. As a result, there was even less sympathy for the concerns of the workers than during the period of local ownership. The need for unionization began to grow in Luzerne County, despite the knowledge that it would be difficult and possibly deadly.

Movements toward organized labor occurred earlier in the Hazleton area than in the Wyoming fields. Because of the mountain barriers, southern Luzerne County had a closer connection to the Schuylkill fields than it did to Wyoming Valley. Since the days of the Molly Maquires, the spirit of worker solidarity against the mine operators was strongest in the lower anthracite region. Nor was unionization a concern to the eastern and southern Europeans when they first came to the coal towns. The Knights of Labor and later, the United Mine Workers, had only limited success in organizing the mine workers of Luzerne County.

Then, in the late summer of 1897, Gomer Jones, a tough Welsh mine superintendent for the Wilkes-Barre and Lehigh Coal Company in the Hazleton area, attempted to cut costs. He proposed to establish a central location for the housing of mules. This would require an extra two hours of unpaid travel time for mule-drivers. Jones' idea was certainly not a popular one. Since most of the mule-drivers were recent immigrants, Gomer Jones became the object of scorn in the Slavic and Italian communities around Hazleton. After a number of altercations with the company, the United Mine Workers began to gain worker support in southern Luzerne County and in the bordering areas of northern Carbon and Schuylkill Counties. By September, a full scale strike led by the new immigrants was underway throughout the anthracite fields. Their demand was the same pay scale as their American counterparts.

During the course of the strike, a group of workers from Harwood planned a march through Hazleton and on to the mines at Lattimer. There they would demonstrate solidarity with the strikers in that patch town north of Hazleton. Luzerne County Sheriff James Martin was alerted. He organized an armed posse of 150 deputies to stop the 300 mostly East European mine workers. The marchers, unarmed and carrying an American flag, reached the dusty company town in the afternoon of Friday, September 10, 1897. There, Martin and some of the lead marchers exchanged words. A fight broke out between Martin and one of the workers. In the midst of this someone yelled, "fire!" A volley of perhaps 150 shots rang out through Lattimer. Men, crying out pleas to God in Slovak, Polish, and Lithuanian, were riddled with bullets from the Winchester rifles. Most were shot in the back as they attempted to escape. When the massacre ceased, at least nineteen men were dead and thirty-two were wounded. Horror, anger and grief swept through Luzerne County. Although Martin and his deputies were tried for murder, they were found not guilty.

If anyone believed that the Lattimer Massacre and the subsequent acquittal of the sheriff and his posse would stem the tide of unionization, they were gravely mistaken. Luzerne County now became a rallying point for the spirit of workers' solidarity in the anthracite fields and throughout America. With workers averaging only 190 days work per year, their pay rarely accumulated to more than $500. It was necessary for wives and children to find hard and sometimes demeaning work in order for the family to survive.

In the early 1900s, led by the charismatic United Mine Workers President Johnny Mitchell, the anthracite workers again challenged the operators. Calling for unity among the diverse, and often disagreeing, new immigrant groups, Mitchell said, "the coal you dig isn't Slavish or Polish or Irish coal, it's coal." He gained the backing of Father John J. Curran, of Wilkes-Barre, and other influential Catholic clergy. In 1902, 140,000 anthracite workers, the greatest number of them from Luzerne County, began "The Great Strike." In the face of

"The boss of the situation. The real gainer of the great strike." An advertisement exposing the labor conflict from the coal strike of 1897.

Luzerne County Sheriff James Martin's deputies who shot down striking miners on Sept. 10, 1897 at Lattimer. Sixteen miners were killed and thirty eight wounded.

The champion proponents in insuring the rights of mine workers and their families. Bishop Michael Hoban, President Theodore Roosevelt and Father John J. Curran, kicking off Roosevelt's "Bull Moose" Campaign in Wilkes-Barre.

As the president of the United Mine Workers Union, John Mitchell was responsible for the resolution of the Great Union Strikes of 1900 and 1902.

Drafted and enlisted men leaving the Hazleton train station for Fort Meade during World War I, Nov. 1917.

hunger, deprivation, and an exodus of people from the region, the mine workers held on to their principles. With a shortage of home heating fuel beginning to affect the urban industrial centers of the east, President Theodore Roosevelt was forced to intervene. On March 22, 1903, over nine months after the strike started, a settlement was reached. The UMW accepted a ten percent wage increase and a nine hour day, as opposed to the twenty percent increase and the eight hour day of its original demands.

There are those who believe that Mitchell sold the mine workers short, while others question how much commitment Roosevelt really felt to the cause of labor. However, some facts can not be questioned. The Great Strike enabled Mitchell to bring the UMW into national prominence. The national perception of Teddy Roosevelt was that he fought for the common man. This helped to make him one of the most popular of American presidents. Luzerne County was the focal point of these major events in American history.

The early 1900s was the prime period of anthracite mining and cultural expansion in Luzerne County. The coming of World War I and the subsequent changes in American society brought major changes to the coal industry and the people whose livelihoods depended upon it. The legacy of this peak industrial era still influences the culture of the county. The hardships endured by the mine families brought about mistrust for large, outside corporations. It is not easy to forget the human and environmental devastation that was inflicted on the county. Also, workers learned that in order to gain respect for their cause, they had to organize. Throughout the twentieth century Luzerne County demonstrated its support for unionization. But while the people of the county challenged the authority of their corporate employers, they also gained a reputation as industrious and dedicated employees.

During this era, only twelve percent of the population lived in Luzerne County's rural regions. Nevertheless, they played an important role in the county's social history. With the development of dairy and truck farms, these agricultural townships served as major food suppliers to the coal towns. The breeding of new types of cattle, and the use of silos for storing their feed year-round, helped lead to the tremendous growth of dairy farming during the late 1800s. The Back Mountain, Mountaintop, Butler Valley, Conyngham Valley, and the lower Susquehanna Valley region became the principal dairy and truck farming regions of the county.

Most of the residents of the rural areas were still Protestants of Connecticut Yankee or Pennsylvania German stock. Although the massive growth of the coal towns increased their markets, many farm dwellers were still suspicious of change. Americans attached much faith to their belief in the yeoman ideal. Farming was seen as the real strength of the nation, and industrialization and all the changes it brought were felt to be detrimental to America. The farmers of Luzerne County were only a few miles away from the industrial transformation of Wyoming Valley and Hazleton. To them the dirty coal towns, the thousands of immigrants, and the emphasis upon corporate wealth threatened to end their way of life. While many of their fears were based on misinformation and prejudice, they were correct in their assumption that farm life in Luzerne County had reached its peak. As with the coal industry, conditions after World War I brought about a decline in agriculture.

The unprecedented industrial development in Luzerne County was reflected in the population growth between 1880 and 1920. In 1880, the county numbered 133,065 people. It grew to 201,203 by 1890, 257,121 in 1900, 343,186 in 1910, and 390,991 in 1920. This is nearly a 300 percent growth rate. Wilkes-Barre became a city in 1872, Hazleton in 1891, and Pittston in 1894. In the century and a half since its founding, Luzerne County had grown from a few frontier settlements to a major urban-industrial center.

The years between 1880 and 1920 were a tumultuous time in Luzerne County. Like America, the county saw the development of large scale industrial development, massive immigration, the growth of organized labor, and increasing concerns over these rapid changes. But as the county was about to enter a new era, people were making compromises and accommodations in order to deal with the changing times.

Advertisement for Miner and Company, manufacturers of flour, feed, grain, and hay, c. 1880.

View of Dallas Corners in 1874.

Joseph Shaver's family purchased large tracts of land in 1812 which became known as Shavertown.

The original Market Street covered bridge as seen from the Kingston side of the Susquehanna River

Wilkes-Barre's Market Street bridge today.

Autumn fishing on Harvey's Lake.

A fall scene in Hollenback Cemetery on River Street in Wilkes-Barre.

Winter scene in the mountains surrounding Luzerne County.

One room school-house in Luzerne.

The Luzerne County Courthouse located on River and North Streets in Wilkes-Barre.

The Martz Pavillion, Kirby Park, in summer. Designed by Bakker and Lewis, Architects.

Hazleton City Hall, Church Street, Hazleton as renovated in 1937 from its original Georgian style to Art Deco.

Shoemaker Mill that once stood on the corner of 8th Street and Shoemaker Avenue in West Wyoming.

Trucksville United Methodist Church.

Luzerne County lake house.

Fall scene in Hollenback Cemetery, Wilkes-Barre.

Harvey's Lake home.

Hanson's Amusement Park, Harvey's Lake, ceased operation in the 1970s and was demolished in 1991.

Hanson's Amusement Park sign.

Wilkes-Barre's Public Square renovation by Bohlin and Powell Architects, 1972.

Summer festival in Kirby Park.

The running track at Kirby Park.

Former Luzerne High School.

Wilkes University playing King's College at the new Monarch Field Complex in Wilkes-Barre.

Ballet Theatre Pennsylvania's production of the Nutcracker at the F.M. Kirby Center for the Performing Arts in Wilkes-Barre.

The Westmoreland Club, the former Shoemaker home, on South Franklin Street, Wilkes-Barre.

The Fred M. and Jessie A. Kirby Episcopal House in Glen Summit.

The old Luzerne/Wilkes-Barre train station.

Early union affiliations were often reinforced by local church groups. Local No. 8 Union of Associated Steam Shovel men with St. John's First Slovak Band of Hazleton.

CHAPTER FOUR

Anthracite and Agriculture

The anthracite industry reached its peak production in 1917, when steady growth following the Great Strike of 1902 combined with a wartime economy to reach a record output of nearly 100 million tons. However, the harbingers of decline were evident immediately following World War I. Much of this decline was related to the use of alternative fuel sources. At a time when many consumers were angered at the continually rising price of anthracite coal, technological advances were being made in the oil and natural gas industries. As a result, these new home heating fuels became both more cost efficient and cleaner. This trend began in the 1920s and continued at an increasing rate until the 1950s.

Coal strike arbitration meeting. John L. Lewis, Thomas McKinnly, and Rev. John J. Curran.

Although the use of alternative fuel sources was the major reason for the decline of coal mining in Luzerne County, other problems within the industry contributed to its downfall. The mine operators were guilty of poor management, and they failed to support research and development that could make anthracite competitive with the new fuels. Along with this, the railroads continued to charge high shipping rates that made the cost of hard coal unfavorable in contrast to oil and natural gas. The successful Populist and Progressive movements had left the mine owners with a negative image. No longer the hero-entrepreneurs of the nineteenth century, they were viewed as profit-hungry, absentee owners, who were willing to sacrifice the lives and livelihoods of their workers.

Labor unrest during the 1920s was also responsible for anthracite's decline. The problem, however, was less one of worker demands than of operator desires. Since the use of non-union labor in the southern Appalachian coal fields had increased, the anthracite operators sought to decrease the power of the United Mine Workers (UMW) in Luzerne County. The owners implemented wage cuts and hoped to curtail collective bargaining rights. To many mine workers it appeared that the operators were turning back the clock on UMW progress. The result was a devastating round of labor strife. During this period the UMW was under the leadership of John L. Lewis.

Lewis was a controversial figure

Mine union negotiators join President Franklin D. Roosevelt aboard his campaign train in 1936. From left, John L. Lewis, FDR, Congressman Patrick Boland, and Marvin McIntyre.

Crews pushing railroad cars into Knox Mine Disaster fissure in an attempt to stop flooding in the shaft.

with a forceful personality and a desire for control of the union locals. At times, he had more success dealing with the operators than with Luzerne County union leaders. The first strike under Lewis' leadership occurred in 1922 and lasted for 163 days. In 1925, a 170 day strike occurred. Although Lewis believed that he guided the UMW to successful settlements in both of these strikes, dissidents in Luzerne County saw them differently. Many Wyoming Valley mine workers felt that Lewis was selling out the anthracite miners in order to gain better relations with the operators.

Much of the insurgence took place in Pittston and Wilkes-Barre. Led by Thomas Maloney, valley miners challenged the UMW by forming a rival union—The United Anthracite Miners of Pennsylvania (UAMP). When the UAMP launched strikes in 1933, violence occurred throughout the Wyoming Valley between UAMP members, loyalists to the UMW who desired to work, the mine operators, and the police. A UAMP member from Larksville was killed while walking the picket line. In Hanover Township a father was fatally shot and his son wounded as the result of a disagreement over the new union. At Plymouth's Nottingham Colliery, five men were wounded and fifty others injured when strikers clashed with police. The D.L.&W. Railroad bridge, connecting Plymouth and Hanover Township, was bombed. A vehicle owned by the daughter of Judge W.A. Valentine, the jurist who sentenced Maloney and twenty-eight others for contempt, was destroyed by dynamite in downtown Wilkes-Barre. Although Mary Valentine was not in the car, a young newsboy was severely injured in the explosion. Only the respected labor advocate and Wilkes-Barre priest, John J. Curran, was able to bring any sort of calm to the troubled area. The work stoppage ended in 1935, when the UAMP was judged illegal by the Labor Relations Board. Maloney received assurances that strikers would be rehired when the need arose. Shortly afterwards, the UAMP disbanded.

Despite settlement of the strike the violence was not over. On Good Friday of 1936, Maloney, his son, and Hanover Township school director Michael Gallagher were murdered by dynamite concealed in cigar boxes. The packages were marked "sample" as if to indicate Easter gifts. Michael Fugmann, a friend of Maloney and a deserter from the German army, was charged with the brutal attacks. Fugmann disavowed any knowledge of the bombings. The Commonwealth based its case on an impressive amount of circumstantial evidence and Fugmann was convicted of first degree murder in the death of Maloney. He was executed in the electric chair. Although at the time some believed that Fugmann was the hapless victim of a UMW or operator conspiracy, scholars now feel that Fugmann was the perpetrator, and his motives were more related to his mental state than to any plot. Whatever the rationale for the labor strife of the 1920s and 1930s, such violence could only accelerate the decline of anthracite mining.

Anthracite mining revived briefly during World War II, but once that conflict ended the move toward alternative fuels continued. By the end of the 1950s only 5,000 men were employed in the anthracite fields, compared to 140,000 in 1900. Underground mining came to an abrupt end in the Wyoming Valley in 1959. Engineers had long warned that removing the sections of coal known as pillars, left behind as supports during the original mining of the area, was courting trouble. This was especially risky when mining in close proximity to the Susquehanna River. However, a number of smaller operations were willing to take such a chance.

These dire predictions were realized at the Knox Coal Company near Pittston. On January 22, 1959, the Susquehanna River crashed through the few remaining feet of rocks separating the mine from the river. Twelve men lost their lives and the river water flooded the vast network of inter-connected tunnels beneath the Wyoming Valley. Attempts to seal the opening were made by diverting railroad gondolas and small mine cars into the fissure. The severity of the situation was realized when the huge gondolas were sucked like toys beneath the swollen river. Although state mine inspectors recommended the prosecution of seven supervisors of the Knox Coal Company and the Pennsylvania Coal Company, a joint Pennsylvania legislative committee stated the negligence was not the fault of any group of people but was the result of "...a chain of events, each link of which was necessary or incidental to the resultant tragedy..." Nonetheless, a series of indictments and guilty verdicts were eventually handed down against six Knox and UMW officials for their role in the hazardous operation of the mine.

Early strip mining operations in Hazleton showing the bucket loader operators and workmen. c. 1900

The flooding of Wyoming Valley's mine tunnels marked the end of underground mining in the center of the region's anthracite industry. Although underground operations continued in the Hazleton area, and surface mining occurred throughout the county, these undertakings were minor in comparison to anthracite's heyday. The monumental impact of the disaster upon operations in the Wyoming Valley made people throughout the region realize that the anthracite industry was virtually dead.

Pollock's Cafe, Main Street, Ashley, located directly across from the Huber Colliery.

The Pioneer No. 1 Volunteer Fire Company, Hazleton, c. 1900.

Major changes in the culture of Luzerne County also took place between 1920 and 1960. During the first decade of this era ethnicity was at its height. Over sixty percent of the county's residents were foreign born or the children of immigrants. In Dupont, for example, nearly ninety percent of the population fell into one of these categories. Ethnic enclaves could be found in every mining community and increasing numbers of immigrants were settling in the county's rural areas. Hundreds of ethnic institutions, such as churches, fraternal organizations, athletic clubs, and even neighborhood taverns, were thriving throughout the county. These institutions were a part of the county's character, giving it a reputation as one of the most ethnically diverse regions in America.

In Plymouth, for example, sections of the town were dominated by specific ethnic groups. The upper end was the home of large numbers of Lithuanians, Slovaks and Poles. East Shawnee Avenue and its side streets had a large Welsh population. Many Irish resided near the center of the town as did those of English ancestry. The lower end was predominantly Polish, Ukrainian, and English. Each group had its own church or churches. While its church was central to each group's identity, other activities had great importance as well. In Plymouth the choral groups and the majority of the vocalists were Welsh. Slavic-Americans operated many small taverns which were central to the fraternal organizations along with their athletic and social events. For example, the Polish Alliance club was the home of a fraternal insurance company, a small tavern, and a large dance hall which hosted both big band and polka orchestras. As in many of the county's communities, Plymouth's Masonic Lodge and its Eastern Star auxiliary were important associations for many of the prominent Protestants. Although organized around a strict fraternal and moral code, these organizations fostered business and social connections.

The Cambrian Glee Club in traditional Welsh costume, 1924.

Despite its prominence in the 1920s, the ethnic culture of Luzerne County was already beginning to change. After World War I, immigration to Luzerne County declined dramatically. The flow was halted on a national level by Congress's passage of immigration restrictions. Nativists, fearful of the large number of foreign-born in the United States, succeeded in securing passage of the Johnson Bill in 1924. This act placed strict quotas on immigrants from eastern and southern Europe. These major sources of migration to Luzerne County were almost completely curtailed. The decline of the anthracite industry also discouraged people from moving to Luzerne County. Consequently, even if immigrants could get into America they would not be inclined to seek work where the opportunities were limited. The lack of potential employment also deterred large numbers of African Americans displaced by agricultural changes in the South from migrating to Luzerne County. In 1930 there were 1032 African-Americans in the county and 877 in Wilkes-Barre. Thus, during the 1920s Great Migration of America's southern Black population the county saw an increase of only 217 African-American residents. By the time of the Great Depression, only a limited number of new arrivals were still seeking homes in Luzerne County.

The absence of new immigrants to Luzerne County was a turning point in the region's social history. For some of the immigrants and many of their offspring, the focus of their lives moved from Old World traditions toward American institutions. As more children of immigrants attended public schools, they got involved in such activities as popular music and scholastic sports. This desire to "Americanize" was a source of tension between the generations. Parents feared that sons and daughters would lose their ethnic culture, while the children sought to forge their own lives apart from Old World traditions. Although their children, and even their grandchildren, continued to adhere to many of the ethnic customs, the 1920s marked the beginning of large scale Americanization. Big band dances and high school football games were as important to the children of immigrants as their ethnic customs and organizations. With the coming of World War II, many of the area's young adults moved away from their ethnic roots to serve in the armed forces or work in wartime industries. Even those who remained in the area were pulled further into the American culture by the radio and, after the war, by television. With such forces impacting upon the local citizens, ethnic institutions

Five generations of an immigrant family, Hazleton, c. 1916.

Anthony Richardson, a Boston Store employee, pictured here in full lodge dress.

Kingston Coal Company children at school, c. 1916.

A music lesson in Hazleton, 1896.

Rowley's Band, Wilkes-Barre, 1907.

Portrait of the Irem Temple Chanters in 1928.

Wilkes-Barre's Bethel A.M.E. Church Choir, 1925.

Grist mill started by the Rittenhouse Brothers, Martin and William, pioneer settlers in Black Creek Township, c. 1810.

were becoming more difficult to maintain.

Despite this trend toward Americanization, prejudice toward immigrants, Catholics, Jews, and African Americans continued. It peaked during the 1920s. Even the Ku Klux Klan boasted a following in the county. Rural areas, where an increasing number of immigrants had found homes, were especially fertile ground. Rallies and cross burnings occurred in the Back Mountain and Huntington Mills areas. Klan activities increased in Dallas with the building of the Roman Catholic College Misericordia. The membership of the Mason's nearby Irem Temple Country Club reportedly offered to assist the Sisters of Mercy in patrolling the college grounds. Many Catholics, who had perceived the Masons as being anti-Catholic, must have been surprised by this gesture. Klan activities were often open and supported by many. When C.A. Tilghman, a Grand Kleagle in the Klan, dedicated a new school in Dallas Township in 1927, nearly 4000 people turned out for his address. The local papers openly noted the activities of the day, including a Klan picnic which was held in nearby Huntsville. The Klan's desire for the protection of "American values" was actually a thinly disguised belief that Catholics, Jews, and African Americans could never become "real Americans." Although many young men in Luzerne County joined the Klan in ignorance, rather than hatred, the very existence of this organization was a sad chapter in the social history of the region.

Much of the discrimination toward Catholics, Jews, and African Americans was more covert. Local clubs, organizations, businesses and employers often had unwritten rules that favored native Protestants. African Americans came to realize that even though segregation did not officially exist in Luzerne County, many businesses, organizations, and even the general population practiced it nonetheless. Although official documentation of such actions is scarce, many older African Americans in the county remember restaurants and taverns where their presence was not welcome. Often the discrimination centered around slurs and stereotypes, ranging from outright offensive comments to ethnic jokes.

There was a backlash to this behavior. Often times Catholics were informed that any connection with a Protestant organization was sinful. One young child was chastised by a priest for attending a party in a Methodist church. A teenage girl was told by a nun that participating in activities at the YWCA was a betrayal of her religious heritage. In a predominantly Catholic public elementary school, Protestant children were excluded from the morning

Rosary session. Such actions resulted from an overriding desire to prevent young people from being swayed to other religions and a deep-seated fear that Americanization would mean the loss of traditions that gave meaning to their lives.

It was through the increased interaction of young people of different ethnic backgrounds that the hatred and prejudice subsided. The Great Depression and World War II made some people realize that Americans of all ethnic backgrounds needed to pull together. However, ethnic divisions did not cease with the end of the anthracite era and discrimination toward non-whites continued beyond 1960, as the final chapter in this book shows.

The rural regions in Luzerne County also experienced a great deal of change between 1920 and 1960. From an economic standpoint there was a large drop in the number of farms and the agricultural output. By 1960 farming was no longer the major enterprise outside of the county's coal towns, and suburbanization was well underway in the former farmlands. Socially, there was a movement from a primarily British American or German American Protestant farming population to one which was more culturally and occupationally diverse.

In 1920 one-fourth of Luzerne County's population resided in rural areas. Over 3,000 farms were in operation. By 1960, although more people lived outside the coal towns, the number of working farms fell to 1,388. Local and national trends occurring after World War II accounted for this change. Large scale agribusiness throughout the United States made it difficult for small, family-owned farms, such as those in Luzerne County, to remain profitable. Improvements in transportation and storage forced local farmers to compete with outside producers for the county's markets. Also, the federal government's subsidies to farmers favored the big producers. In addition to these

Lape's ice wagon, Shickshinny, 1900.

nationwide changes, the weak local economy also worked against the county's farmers. The decline of anthracite and the subsequent outmigration left the farmers with a dwindling market. It became more prudent to sell their operation to developers than to plunge further into debt.

Huntington Dairy, Inc., Shickshinny, c. 1960.

The cultural shift in rural Luzerne County was underway prior to the large scale decline in agriculture. By the 1920s many immigrants had saved enough money as coal miners to purchase or lease a farm. Some continued to labor in the mines while tending their farms, while others went into agriculture full-time. Whatever their employment status, for the first time in history the rural regions of Luzerne County had a

Wright and Mann's grocery store, Hazleton, 1896.

Acme Market, Shickshinny, 1961.

The Hazleton Mercantile Co., c. 1920.

Portrait of a Ukrainian family that settled in Hazleton, c. 1919.

Aerial view of Shickshinny and Mocanaqua in the 1950s.

The Streamline Aerocycle made by Henry Platt, Hazleton.

culturally diverse population. Poles migrated from Nanticoke, Plymouth, and Wilkes-Barre to Mocanaqua, Lake Silkworth, Fairmount Springs, and Dorrance. Here they founded ethnic Catholic parishes in the center of Methodist, Baptist, Lutheran, and Reformed areas. Lithuanians settled in the Hunlock Creek area, Slovaks in Mocanaqua, and Ukrainians moved to the Back Mountain. While the presence of these new arrivals created such repercussions as the Ku Klux Klan and nativism, some rural dwellers felt that the relatively equal occupational levels of Luzerne County's farmers resulted in a lower tension level than that in the coal towns. This was especially true during the Depression and World War II when farmers of all ethnic backgrounds saw a greater need for cooperation. Immigrant children tended to become Americanized more rapidly in rural areas. Because the ethnic population was small and scattered, young people could not form cliques based upon ethnicity.

Social change took a different turn in the post-World War II era. As farmers went out of business, real estate developers began building suburban communities in the Back Mountain, Mountaintop, Bear Creek, and the Conyngham Valley. Both professional people and industrial workers left the crowded conditions and potential for mine subsidence in the coal towns in favor of the more pastoral setting of these new suburbs. Some of the earliest developments were Chase Manor in Jackson Township and Oak Hill in Lehman Township. Many suburban residents continued to work in the urban centers Wilkes-Barre or Hazleton. However, as the population shifted the 1950s saw new businesses beginning to appear in areas that were previously farmland, although this trend did not peak until after 1960.

In Luzerne County, as throughout America, technological advances led to a new era in communication, transportation, and household conveniences. By the 1930s, telephones were commonplace and radios linked all parts of the nation. Motion picture houses appeared throughout the county. Automobiles arrived to supplement the vast array of train and streetcar services. Washing machines and iceboxes began to change the role of homemakers.

While most Luzerne County residents were aware of these changes, few were able to enjoy their full benefits. In the coal towns and on

The Wilkes-Barre Railway Corporation Parade float (1924) with a replica of the first electric railroad car from 1888.

The Weiss Garage and Nash Automobile Sales showing cars and commercial vehicles in Hazleton in the 1930s.

the farms telephones were regarded as a luxury. Neighbors often relied upon one family's phone to receive any important messages. The radio, however, was more commonplace. Perhaps it was this device more than any other that brought the American popular culture to the area. By way of network hook-ups local residents shared the news, drama, comedy, and sports with millions of other Americans. Motion pictures also pulled the region into the larger American culture. Along with millions of other Americans, moviegoers in the county watched Rudolph Valentino and Mary Pickford. Although the automobile was becoming more common, most county residents relied on trains, streetcars, and walking as their means of transportation. While farmers were increasingly viewing the truck as a necessity, the automobile did not become an essential item for urban dwellers until after World War II.

Luzerne County was swept into the American mania of popular sports during the 1920s. Although professional baseball and boxing were popular in the area, it was high school athletics that really captured the region's fancy. Some of the most powerful athletic squads in Pennsylvania's scholastic sport history were found in Luzerne County during the 1920s and 1930s.

Football reached almost fanatical proportions. In Wyoming Valley the Big Four—Wilkes-Barre (later Coughlin), Kingston, Plymouth and Nanticoke High Schools—dominated the gridiron scene. By the 1930s, Larksville, G.A.R. and Meyers were also in the thick of the championship chase. Hazleton High School established itself as a power in the Lower Anthracite region, where their team faced such opponents as

The Lattimer Street Car of the Hazleton Railroad, c. 1920.

Hazleton Opera House in 1896.

Opening of the new Comerford Motion Picture Theatre, Public Square, Wilkes-Barre, 1938.

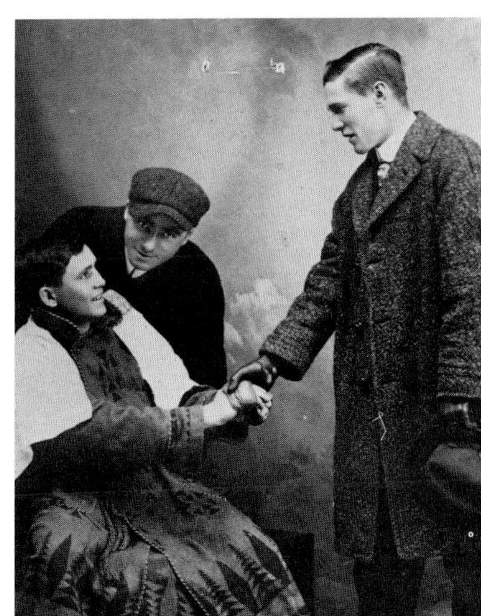

Hazleton prize fighter, Johnny Mahony, c. 1930.

NANTICOKE: THOSE CHAMPIONSHIP SEASONS

Although many scholastic athletic teams gained prominence, it was Nanticoke High School's basketball team that first brought a state championship to Luzerne County. Beginning with its first crown in 1923, Nanticoke became legendary for its prowess on the court.

High school sports were just gaining popularity when Coach Francis McDermott guided the Nans to a victory over Harrisburg Tech in 1923 in what was only the third Pennsylvania Interscholastic Athletic Association (PIAA) championship. The outpouring of support increased when the squad journeyed to Chicago for the National Playoffs. After defeating a team from Montana the Nans were beaten by a South Carolina school.

Under new coach Dick Leary, the 1924 and 1925 teams captured the District II championships. With each new success press coverage of the Nans increased. When the 1926 team went through the regular season with twenty-one straight victories, they were dubbed the "Wonder Five" and considered to be one of the best teams in the nation. Nanticoke played in front of capacity crowds on their way to the state championship. With a state victory over Erie Tech the Nans gained another trip to the National Playoffs in Chicago. The city of Nanticoke was whipped into a frenzy. Game results were wired back to the State Theatre and "Main Street was black with people" awaiting the results. Although Nanticoke was defeated in the quarter-finals, their reputation as a basketball power was secure. Perhaps more importantly, basketball served as a unifying force in a town with deep ethnic, religious, economic, and labor divisions.

The economic downturn in the anthracite region was reflected in the dearth of Luzerne County teams in the state playoffs. No high school ever won a state championship when their town was suffering economic hardships. That is why the 1961 Nanticoke state championship was so important. Under the able leadership of Coach Syl Bozinski, the Nans gave inspiration and hope to a town in the midst of unemployment and out-migration. With each victory over larger and more affluent schools, the community pride grew. After their championship victory over Hickory Township, thousands greeted the young men during the course of a twenty-mile parade. It was not just the people of Nanticoke that honored the squad but citizens from throughout a county hit hard by the decline of anthracite.

Aerial view of Nanticoke in the 1960s.

In 1966 Nanticoke High School was absorbed by the Greater Nanticoke Area School District. Community pride once again swelled when the 1990 girls basketball team under Rose Volpicelli won the PIAA state championship.

While it is argued that too much emphasis can be placed on scholastic sport, it can not be denied that sports brought a town together when it needed it the most.

Mount Carmel, Shamokin and Pottsville.

The extent of this local involvement in scholastic football is shown by the fact that for important games, professional bookmakers set odds that were often published in the newspapers. In 1928, when Larksville High School began to challenge the Big Four, the team received considerable publicity in all the local papers. But when the school district's teachers finally were paid after a five month delay, the event rated an article of about one-hundred words in one daily. The 1928 Plymouth-Nanticoke Thanksgiving Day game created the greatest frenzy of all. Prior to the game there was a long list of ticket reservations and a warning was issued that bogus tickets were likely to appear. Admission was one dollar and the paid attendance was 13,583. Since the combined population of the communities was approximately 42,000, and considering few tickets were sold to outside fans, this means that over one-third of residents in the two communities witnessed the contest. Translated to current figures and conditions, this would amount to over 25,000 fans paying roughly ten dollars to see Wyoming Valley West go against Greater Nanticoke Area. When Kingston won the unofficial state championship in 1936, local scholastic football reached its pre-World War II pinnacle.

Luzerne County was also a dominant force in the state's scholastic basketball scene in the 1920s and 1930s. During this time the anthracite region produced eight state champions, of which six were from Luzerne County. With championships in 1928, 1929 and 1938, Hazleton had more crowns than any other school in Pennsylvania prior to World War II. Nanticoke captured championships in 1923 and 1926, and Newport Township gained honors in 1936.

The impact of high school athletics was tremendous in Luzerne County. Since most school districts encompassed a single municipality, the high school teams were the focus of commu-

The South Side Y.M.C.A. Tennis Club, Wilkes-Barre, 1928.

Plymouth Public High School football team, 1903.

The champion girls basketball team of Freeland High School, 1929.

The championship basketball team of Edwardsville, 1932.

First official basketball team at Plymouth High School, 1904.

nity pride and identification. For the first time since the period of great immigration, the diverse residents in each town came together for a common purpose. Scholastic sports contributed to the movement from an ethnically oriented society to one that was more community based. But they also fostered localism and competitiveness between the communities. Residents often saw the preservation of their town's identity as more important than the countywide cooperation needed to modernize the political and educational systems. The resistance to such changes will be further discussed in Chapter Five.

The stock market crash of 1929 and the onset of the Great Depression caused county residents to turn their attention to the worldwide economic crisis. Because of the severe slowdown in the anthracite industry during the 1920s, Luzerne County's residents were in many ways better prepared than the rest of the nation to deal with want and sacrifice. Still, the catastrophic extent of the Depression took its toll on the county. County relief rolls totalled 85,711 and nearly 2,000 homeless and transients roamed the area. "Hoovervilles" and hobo camps could be found on the outskirts of many coal towns. One of the largest hobo camps was located near the site of the present-day Narrows Shopping Center in Edwardsville.

Homeowners and farmers, unable to pay rent, mortgages, or property taxes, were forced to leave their homes. An increased number of people were arrested for stealing coal. In 1934, for example, eleven persons were charged with theft after an altercation with police in Wilkes-Barre Township. Many people worked without a regular salary. Some did so as an exchange for payment on their real estate taxes. Others, such as teachers in Pittston Township and Pringle, worked for long periods without pay to prevent the financial collapse of their school districts.

The election of Franklin Delano Roosevelt and his New Deal brought hope to Luzerne County. While his programs and other state related actions did not bring an end to the Depression, they did stabilize the economy and raise the morale of the people. New Deal work programs, such as the Civil Works Administration (CWA), Public Works Administration (PWA), and the Works Progress Administration (WPA), brought much needed jobs and money to the region. The CWA employed over 13,000 while the WPA provided work for more than 16,000. As much as $8,000,000 in yearly wages was distributed to county workers through New Deal programs. Although Luzerne County farmers received little from the Agricultural Adjustment Act (AAA) subsidies, they did gain a share from the subsequent Agricultural Conservation Program (ACP). Through it, 1,196 county farmers obtained an average of $63.68 in ACP allotments. Perhaps the biggest benefit to the small dairy farmers and dairy operators of the county was the creation of the state Milk

The battleship Arizona shortly after the attack on Pearl Harbor, Hawaii, December 7, 1941.

The inauguration of airline passenger service to Wilkes-Barre in 1929.

Control Commission by Governor George H. Earle. This stabilized milk prices and prevented many small farmers and dairy operators from falling victim to a price war.

Roosevelt's action gained him widespread support with the urban and ethnic voters of the county. In 1936 he had a 104,809 to 81,672 margin of victory over Alf Landon, the Republican challenger. Roosevelt captured all six of the county's legislative districts. However, the rural Protestants were distrustful of the New Deal and remained firmly behind the Republican Party. In the rural, non-mining municipalities Landon had a 12,086 to 8,240 voting edge.

Despite the ominous nature of the onset of World War II in Europe, it brought some economic recovery for county residents. As the United States moved toward a wartime economy, the region's mines, mills, and factories experienced an upswing in employment. Other county residents found employment in defense plants in New Jersey, Connecticut, Ohio, and the Philadelphia and Washington, D.C. areas. In each of these regions there were enclaves of "coal crackers" from the anthracite counties.

When the United States entered the war after the Japanese attack on Pearl Harbor, the residents of Luzerne County became immersed in the conflict. While many volunteered for service, it was still necessary to utilize the draft. Selective Service offices, located in most of the larger towns in the county, presided over the drafting and induction of the young men who were called to serve. Over 55,000 county residents served in the armed services and more than 1,500 men and women made the supreme sacrifice. Many recall the dreaded sight of the Western Union man walking toward a home with a telegram informing a family of a loved one's death.

On the home front the men and women in the mines, factories, and textile mills made products necessary for the war effort. There was now work in the county for almost anyone who desired employment.

Victory committee honoring the African American veterans of World War II in Wilkes-Barre, December 1945.

This was especially true for women. With the large number of men in uniform and the presence of a traditionally female employment structure in the garment and textile industries, local women had many job opportunities. An advertisement for Joy Tyme Frocks in Lee Park read: "50 Girls, No Experience Necessary, Defense Work." Other area workers opted for the more lucrative jobs in the large defense plants in New Jersey, Connecticut, or the Philadelphia area. These out-of-town employers, familiar with the strong work ethic in the coal regions, often placed classified advertisements in area newspapers and arranged for transportation to the factory site. Almost every family had someone who migrated from the county for wartime employment. Since the manufacturing of consumer goods was curtailed, gasoline, sugar, meat and other commodities were rationed. Most people readily accepted these restrictions, understanding that rationing helped the war effort and prevented hoarding and high prices. Residents prided themselves on the ingenuity displayed in getting the most out of their rationed food and fuel. Despite the high level of patriotism in Luzerne County, a black market existed where, for a price, rationed goods could be obtained without the proper coupons. In almost every town the senior citizens can still recall who was involved in war profiteering.

With the end of World War II came America's unprecedented economic prosperity. But the decline of the anthracite industry excluded the people of Luzerne County from this national trend. By 1950 more than 21,000, or twelve percent, were unemployed in the county. By 1958 the unemployment rate was a staggering 16.9 percent and this figure would most likely have been higher if it were not for the GI Bill's education programs. As a result, outmigration continued at a tremendous rate. In 1940 the county's population was 441,518. By 1950 it had fallen to 391,226 and ten years later there were only 346,972 residents. When the Knox Disaster brought an end to much of the county's anthracite mining in 1959, it was a disheartened county that faced the future.

Mining's decline also saw a shift in employment trends. Throughout the 1900s an increasing number of garment factories and textile mills began operating in the region. By the 1950s these businesses were the leading employers in the county. The majority of their workers were women, and approximately 12,000 found employment in the county's nearly 300 garment and textile operations. Consequently, the phenomenon of large numbers of women in the work force occurred in Luzerne County earlier than most areas of the country. In many families women were the principal wage-earners. As with their male counterparts in the workforce, a strong spirit of unionism prevailed in the factories and mills. The International Ladies Garment Workers Union (ILGWU) became a powerful force in the region's labor activities.

During the very worst of the economic depths, there were indications that the county could recover. In both the Wilkes-Barre and Hazleton areas economic revitalization plans were well underway during the 1950s. Increased educational opportunities became available for the generation coming of age in the 1940s and 1950s. King's College was founded in 1946 and the following year Bucknell Junior College, first established in 1933, was chartered as Wilkes College (now Wilkes

ESTHER J. TINSLEY ONE WOMAN'S WORK

Esther J. Tinsley was appointed administrator of the Pittston Hospital in 1913, at a time when few women were entrusted with responsible leadership positions. During her more than 50 years of service, her work ranged from providing care during disasters to advancements in nursing education. Tinsley was praised for her work in three major crises. In 1918, when the influenza epidemic swept though the region, she initiated full-scale emergency operations to deal with the disease. Two years later, Tinsley's efforts in caring for the injured in the Laurel Line electric train wreck were officially lauded by the League of Women Voters. And decades later, the Radio, TV and Press Association of Lackawanna County honored her for her calm and efficient handling of the patients, the public, and the press in the aftermath of the 1959 Knox Mine Disaster.

Tinsley was a leader in establishing high standards for the nursing profession. She worked tirelessly for the creation and certification of nursing schools and their graduates and held a number of offices in professional organizations. Tinsley also founded the Red Cross chapter in Pittston. Along with all of these activities in her field she also had a strong commitment to public service as a leader in local civic and social welfare associations. When she died in 1981, Esther Tinsley's contribution to the health and well-being of county residents was monumental.

University). Along with the previously established College Misericordia, the county now had three baccalaureate degree granting institutions. The Pennsylvania State University campuses in Hazleton and Wilkes-Barre, established prior to World War II, expanded rapidly after the war with the enrollment of GIs. Although many of the graduates of these schools left the area, those who remained provided the core of the technical and professional positions needed for recovery.

The residents of Luzerne County who came of age during this period were accustomed to want and sacrifice. They had lived through a long-term decline in the local economy, the Great Depression, and World War II. Such circumstances had to affect those who are now the county's senior citizens. They are often a very cautious group, who believe that hard work is necessary to gain even the smallest of rewards. As a group who grew up giving so much to family and country, they will often live frugally themselves but bestow generously upon others, especially their children and grandchildren. In order to fully understand the people of present-day Luzerne County, one must appreciate this older generation's experience of want and sacrifice.

With the demise of anthracite, the Americanization of the large ethnic population, and the decline of agriculture, Luzerne County was a very different place in 1960 than it was in 1920. Despite what appeared to be a bleak future, the region showed incredible resilience and ambition.

Woman at work in the Eberhard-Faber plant in the Crestwood Industrial Park.

Workers and engineers pose for a photograph at the Lattimer Shops, c. 1930.

CHAPTER FIVE

Legacy of the Past, Hope for the Future

Decaying coal breakers like the Huber Breaker in Ashley, represent the last remnants of a once thriving economic force in Luzerne County.

Luzerne County's recent history has been marked by increasing diversification and change in its social and economic systems. With migration out of the county, the arrival of new cultural groups, assimilation of the turn-of-the-century immigrant families, and suburbanization, the social make-up of the region has taken on a new look. Simultaneously, the loss of its dominant industry, a nearly one hundred thousand population decrease, and a twelve percent unemployment rate, has made the economic revitalization of Luzerne County a formidable task.

Luzerne County's class structure, at one time linked to ethnic heritage, has relaxed during the modern era. Although a number of old families still have a great deal of economic influence in the region, wealth and power are now in the hands of people representing various cultural and religious backgrounds. This resulted from two factors. First, as the culture of the immigrants and their children became more American, the base of power began to shift from within the ethnic group to the community or region as a whole. With the help of the GI Bill, higher education and advanced training reached a wider spectrum of the population, opening up more opportunity for social and economic mobility to the children and grandchildren of the immigrants. The second factor was the decreased importance of one's job status in the extremely hierarchical anthracite industry. As the coal industry declined, social and economic status were no longer determined solely by one's role in the

Display for the opening of the Eberhard Faber Factory in the Crestwood Industrial Park.

Members of the Luzerne County Court in the early 1960s. Left to right (first row), Judges Bigelow, Lewis, Pinola, Jones; (second row), Judges Brominski, Lopatto, (Federal Judge) Sheridan, and Schiffman.

Luzerne County Medical Society Annual Dinner, 1979, with Drs. Ehrhart, Buckey, Burns, Drapiewski, Janjigian and Ushinski.

mines, where the newest and least skilled immigrants traditionally occupied the lowest economic rung.

Although the demise of anthracite had a devastating effect on the local economy, it forced industrial diversification. When this was combined with the greater availability of education and training programs, opportunities increased for ambitious and intelligent workers to better themselves.

In the past, men had an obligation to work in the mines in order to support their families. Without the coal industry it was necessary for them to seek alternative employment. Although many suffered because of the lack of decent jobs, others benefited by being forced to look further afield for alternative employment.

As a result of these changes, professions such as law, business, and medicine were no longer dominated by the old families. Politics and education, once controlled by those of Welsh and English heritage, had diversified by the 1960s. Irish, Slavs, Jews, and Italians gained power and influence throughout the county. Although family name and wealth still counted, entrepreneurial skills, education, and ambition began to play a larger role. As a result people from all ethnic and religious backgrounds became social, economic, and political power brokers in the county.

By 1968, descendants of the English served in only three Luzerne County political offices, while Irish and Slovak descendants occupied two offices each. The others were held by a Polish, Italian, German, and Welsh descendant. Two judges of Polish heritage, and one each of Irish, Jewish, Lithuanian, and Welsh heritage comprised the Luzerne County bench.

In Luzerne County's professions ethnic diversity was well established during this period. In 1979, the officers of the Luzerne County Medical Society were of Jewish, Italian, Slovak, Polish, German, Lebanese, Irish, and English heritage. The county's largest law firm was comprised of partners whose ancestry was Italian, Irish, Jewish, German, English, and Lebanese. By the 1970s, the Wilkes-Barre Area School District's principals were of Irish, Polish, German, English, Italian, Slovak, and Welsh background.

Economic recovery and development has been key to Luzerne County's recent history. As mentioned in Chapter Four, immediately following World War II there were those in both the Wilkes-Barre and Hazleton areas who recognized the need to diversify the regional industrial base. William O. Sword's leadership of the Committee of 100, the Industrial Fund, and the Chamber of Commerce, set the pace in Wyoming Valley. In Hazleton, revitalization was spearheaded by the Community Area New Development Organization, with its fitting acronym, CAN-DO.

Although local residents were the driving force behind these efforts, they were greatly aided by an infusion of state and federal money into the anthracite region. The Pennsylvania Industrial Development Corporation loaned nearly 30 million dollars to the area as a whole. Funds from Washington came from a variety of sources, including the Appalachian Regional Development Act and the Public Works and Economic Development Act. In Luzerne County, the Economic Development Council of

CAN-DO AND THE REVITALIZATION OF THE HAZLETON AREA

View of the Valmont Industrial Park in Hazleton, 1980.

When alternative energy sources and highly mechanized surface mining operations drastically decreased employment in the underground mines during the post-World War II era, the Hazleton area was particularly hard hit. In many ways lower Luzerne County's social and economic structure revolved around anthracite even more than Wyoming Valley's. While most communities in the valley were economically viable prior to the coal era, for many Hazleton area towns the only reason for their existence was coal mining, evidenced by the large number of company towns located within Black Creek, Foster, and Hazle townships. The CAN-DO economic revitalization program transformed these potential ghost towns of the declining coal region into a viable, small-scale industrial area.

The veterans returning from World War II took the first action to revitalize the area. Many of the men had been employed in the mines prior to their service, and their homecoming to Hazleton was spoiled by the loss of their former livelihoods. Under the leadership of Fred Bachman, M.L. Blum, Martin Apfelbaum, and Louis Felma, the Greater Hazleton Veterans Association was formed. Their mission was to organize those people in Hazleton who were in a position to create new jobs.

In 1947, the businesses still vital enough to be a part of the Hazleton Chamber of Commerce established the non-profit Hazleton Industrial Development Corporation (HIDC) to attract new industries to lower Luzerne County. The agency collected $650,000 and campaigned aggressively to bring the Electric Auto-Light Corporation, an automotive parts manufacturer from Toledo, Ohio, to a proposed 175,000 square foot plant on Poplar Street. It was hoped that Auto-Light would provide as many as a thousand jobs. However, problems ocurred with the deed to the land, and a labor stoppage delayed construction. As a result Auto-Light was able to provide only one-third of the jobs originally planned.

To Hazletonians, Auto-Light was to be the impetus for a new age of economic development. This apparent failure dashed community morale, but the organizers learned valuable lessons regarding economic planning.

A second venture to recruit a major manufacturer also met with problems. In 1953, $100,000 was raised to bring a Chicago hospital furniture maker, the Sleeprite Corporation, to a 50,000 square foot building in Hazleton. Sleeprite declared bankruptcy in 1956, but all was not lost. A New York dress manufacturing company acquired the bulding and provided over two hundred jobs. Most of the employees in the garment industry were women, however, and the problem of the unemployed coal miners still existed. By 1955 coal production had diminished to fifty percent of its 1920 levels. The unemployment picture got even worse that year when 1,600 workers lost their jobs because of the mine flooding generated by Hurricane Diane. Despite these efforts by the community, migration to other parts of the country seemed to be the only answer for many of the unemployed.

During these difficult years a new attempt at revitalization was made under the strong leadership of Dr. Edgar L. Dessen, a prominent radiologist and president of the Hazleton Chamber of Commerce. Dessen's "Operation Jobs" provided area businesses with red pails for patrons and workers to contribute their dimes, involving the whole community in fund-raising for economic development. A "Mile of Dimes," asked residents to complete a line-up of dimes between Laurel and Wyoming Streets. These undertakings raised $14,000.

Then Pennsylvania Governor George Leader created the Pennsylvania Industrial Development Authority (PIDA), to assist declining coal areas in attracting new industries through low interest state loans. Dessen convinced the Chamber of Commerce of the need for an agency in Hazleton to work with the PIDA.

When skeptics doubted the chances of recovery, Dessen countered by coining the term "CAN-DO" for the new organization. The words for the acronym, Community Area New Development Organization came later. A fundraising goal of $500,000 was set. CAN-DO's two divisions sought contributions from financial institutions and businesses, and sold bonds to the community at large.

Dessen made certain that the bylaws of CAN-DO linked the agency directly with the Chamber of Commerce. He was its fundraising czar, and aggressive tactics were implemented, such as publishing the donor names and the amounts contributed in the Hazleton Standard-Speaker, and announcing them on local radio stations. And underreporting goal totals was not uncommon. Within three weeks CAN-DO exceeded its goal by accumulating $540,000 in bond sales and $200,000 in cash contributions. Dessen was personally responsible for raising one-third of the donations. Learning from the Auto-Light undoing, it was decided that any money raised would not be given directly to the businesses the Chamber hoped to attract. Instead funds would be used to construct buildings that could be sold or leased to new businesses. CAN-DO purchased a 550 acre tract of land near Route 93 owned by Henry Fox, Sr. Fox, a strong supporter of economic revitalization, sold the land at well below market value.

Both Dessen and Fox were concerned about adequate environmental protection and placed restrictions on the types of industries that could locate on the land. This step was unusual during the 1950's and placed these two visionaries well ahead of their time. After a public contest the new facility was named the Valmont Industrial Park.

Dr. Dessen did much of the work in attracting new businesses. General Foam Corporation was the first company to locate at Valmont, and the 1950's ended with six companies established in the park and a second successful fund drive that netted $519,000.

Despite these successes there was a major problem with the relatively poor transportation systems to the region. CAN-DO officials were able to remedy this by their active campaigning for the construction of Interstate Routes 80 and 81 near the Valmont facility. In addition, services at the Hazleton Municipal Airport were expanded. These transportation systems became an integral part of the industrial park's continued growth.

Hazleton was awarded "All-American City" status by the National Municipal League and Look Magazine in 1963, and such major publications as The New York Times, Time, and Newsweek heaped accolades on the city. By that time fifteen new businesses employing 4,000 people had relocated to the Hazleton area. Not resting on its laurels, CAN-DO acquired 1,100 acres in Hazle Township in 1966, and Humboldt Industrial Park was created. This site saw a great deal of additional growth in the 1970's and 1980's.

The efforts of Dr. Dessen and of CAN-DO's dedicated workers were, to a very large degree, responsible for the economic salvation of a dying city and its outlying towns. The Hazleton area's exciting revitalization is one of the most remarkable success stories in Luzerne County's long history.

Northeastern Pennsylvania implemented these federally funded programs.

Credit must go to Congressman Daniel J. Flood for Luzerne County's benefitting so generously from these grants. "Dapper Dan" was described by syndicated columnist Jack Anderson as "sport(ing) a twirled mustache and dress(ing) like the late Adolphe Menjou in a rugged district where a fancy mustache and a dude get-up must be defended with fists." Flood first served in the House of Representatives in 1944. Defeated in 1946, he regained his seat in 1948 and retained it in 1950. After another loss in 1952, he was victorious in every election until his resignation in 1978. With his influential position on the House Appropriations Committee, Flood was a powerful force in Washington during the 1960s and 1970s. His ability to gain funding for the economically depressed region became legendary.

Patterned after revitalization programs in other parts of the country, the Hazleton area and Wyoming Valley plans were successful in securing economic recovery. Two major industrial parks, Valmont and Crestwood, were established, attracting such major employers as RCA and Eberhard-Faber.

The construction of major highway systems served as an incentive for businesses to locate in the county. The Northeast Extension of the Pennsylvania Turnpike connected the county with the Philadelphia area, while the intersection of Interstates 80 and 81 earned the appellation "Crossroads of the East."

Perhaps the most telling story is told by the unemployment figures. From a high of 16.8 percent in 1958, unemployment dropped to 7.9 percent in 1964 and to only 3.9 percent in 1969. These statistics were amazing for a region that many had pronounced economically dead a decade before.

The recovery was not without drawbacks. Most of the jobs created were blue collar laborer positions with wage levels below the state average. Critics believed that the county was simply trading the mining jobs for another type of relatively low paying employment, while local college graduates were still being forced to leave the region to find appropriate work. Teachers, young business executives, and other professionals faced a dim local job market and migrated to the New York/New Jersey, Philadelphia, and Washington metropolitan areas.

Unfortunately, instead of cooperation during this critical period between the various areas in the anthracite region, a sense of competition evolved. Rivalry for government money and industrial expansion developed between the Hazleton area, Wyoming Valley, and Scranton. According to anthropologist and regional planner Dan Rose, Hazleton was the most aggressive in its recovery efforts. This competition did little to ease the long standing conflict between the Hazleton area and Wyoming Valley.

Aerial view of West Nanticoke along the flooding Susquehanna River and Route 11, 1972.

In the midst of this economic revival, disaster struck Luzerne County's most populous area. On June 23, 1972, the Susquehanna River overflowed the flood protection system in Wyoming Valley. The

View taken during the flood of 1972 following the wrath of Tropical Storm Agnes.

Spring of 1972 had already been exceptionally wet. With over fifteen inches of rainfall recorded, small streams were approaching flood stage when the situation was aggravated by Tropical Storm Agnes. Having wreaked havoc along the east coast, on June 21 the storm

Flood cleanup operations on South Main Streeet in Wilkes-Barre, 1972.

stalled over central New York and eastern Pennsylvania. For two days rain drenched the region and sporadic flooding was reported throughout Pennsylvania and New York. The combination of heavy rains and an already saturated watershed caused Wilkes-Barre river levels to rise dramatically. On June 21 the official level in Wilkes-Barre was a shallow 4.47 feet. The next day, Thursday, the reading was 10.03 feet at 10:00 A.M. and 13.67 feet at 4:00 P.M. Although there was general concern, the thirty-seven foot flood protection system offered reassurance to valley residents. However, as many people went to sleep that Thursday evening, the usually docile Susquehanna River went out of control.

At 10:00 P.M. the river levels reached 20.98 and soon after that General Frank Townend, the county's Civil Defense Director, took action. The first evacuation orders were issued in Plymouth. At 2:00 A.M. on June 23, the river was at 29.03 and Nesbitt Hospital and Mercy Hospital began evacuation. Throughout the night, residents of the low lying regions of the valley received news of the impending flood. Some heard it on an emergency radio or television broadcast, while others got the news from friends or from emergency workers relaying evacuation orders.

As dawn broke that Friday, the river reached over thirty-three feet. General Townend called for volunteers to sandbag the dikes bordering Kirby Park, in a desperate and quite possibly dangerous effort to increase the levee protection. By 10:00 A.M. the river was over thirty-seven feet, and forty minutes later Townend called off the sandbagging effort. Sirens wailed throughout Wilkes-Barre at 11:14 A.M. signaling the greatest natural disaster in the history of Luzerne County. Less than two hours later the river broke through in Forty Fort, unearthing the graves at that community's cemetery. Shortly thereafter, the waters came through at Nanticoke, Kingston, and Wyoming. At 7:00 p.m. on June 24, the Susquehanna River crested at 40.60 feet.

Wyoming Valley had seen major flooding in the past, most recently in 1936. However, none compared to the physical and psychological damage caused by the 1972 flood. From Exeter Township in the north to

Salem and Nescopeck Townships in the south, the river valley of Luzerne County was inundated. Over 100,000 people were forced to find shelter in evacuation centers or with friends and relatives. Damage estimates were placed at one billion dollars. Amazingly, only four lives were lost.

When residents were allowed to return after the waters subsided, they were shocked by the condition of their homes and businesses. Some buildings had been washed off their foundations, and many were damaged beyond repair. At best, the structures were filled with mud that destroyed the furnishings and much of the interior. Amid tears and anguish residents wondered how they would ever again rebuild.

At first recovery was slow, confusing and frustrating. Although 68,000 tons of debris were hauled out of the valley each day, many flood victims were unable to get the necessary assistance. Throughout July, emergency centers remained crowded as 9,000 families awaited mobile homes. The $1.7 billion Agnes Recovery Act was seen as inadequate to cover the damages in Luzerne County alone, not to mention the rest of the affected areas along the Susquehanna. Confusion reigned with regard to the amounts and terms of individual government loans.

Anger peaked at a press conference on August 8, with Secretary of Housing and Urban Development (HUD) George Romney, at Wilkes-Barre's Daniel J. Flood Elementary School. Present were members of the Flood Victims Action Council, led by Min Matheson. Tempers flared and the Nixon Administration was accused of inaction. Romney responded in a less than diplomatic manner and a shouting match ensued. The angry HUD Secretary left the rostrum to the jeering of local flood victims.

Despite this poor start, recovery efforts eventually began to take shape. Once again Dan Flood was at the forefront. Using his considerable clout in Washington he secured both emergency relief services and long term financial assistance for home and business owners. The sixty-eight year old congressman seemed to be everywhere as he claimed "this is going to be one Flood against another." Harkening back to his youthful days as an actor, he relished the center stage. Combining his flair for drama and political savvy, Flood cut through the Washington bureaucracy's red tape while directing the day to day recovery efforts in Wilkes-Barre. As Miller and Sharpless note in *The Kingdom of Coal*, the extent of Flood's control was unprecedented for a congressman. Even questions of legality were secondary to the goal of total recovery. Perhaps his greatest accomplishment was the speedy passage of the Small Business Administration (SBA) loan program. These loans carried a one percent interest rate and a $5,000 forgiveness clause, and provided the

The Pennsylvania National Guard constructed temporary bridges, like this one in Shickshinny to replace those damaged or washed away by the flood.

Daniel J. Flood unloading relief supplies for victims of the Agnes Flood.

DANIEL J. FLOOD

Congressman Daniel J. Flood, 1955.

The modern era of Wyoming Valley, and indeed Luzerne County and northeastern Pennsylvania, is defined by Congressman Daniel John Flood (1903-1994). Born in Hazleton on November 26, 1903, "Dapper Dan" attended the public schools of Wilkes-Barre, Pennsylvania, and Florida Military Academy in St. Augustine, Florida. He graduated from Syracuse University, attended Harvard Law School, and graduated from the Dickinson School of Law in Carlisle, Pennsylvania, in 1929.

Admitted to the practice of law in Wilkes-Barre in 1930, Flood was attorney for the Home Owners' Loan Corporation in 1934-35, as well as deputy attorney general for the Commonwealth of Pennsylvania and counsel for the Pennsylvania Liquor Control Board from 1935-39. Within the Democratic Party he became national committeeman for Pennsylvania of the Young Democratic Clubs of America in 1942 and 1943. In 1945 he was named Special Ambassador to Peru by President Truman, and in 1948 was part of the Congressional committee investigating Nazi mass murders of the Polish army. In 1959 he was declared "Public Enemy Number One" by the Republic of Panama Assembly because he favored U.S. sovereignty.

Despite several defeats he served almost seventeen full terms as representative from the Eleventh Congressional District between 1944 and 1980. Then, at 76 years of age and in frail health, he was forced to resign after pleading guilty to conspiracy. Flood agreed to this plea bargain, avoiding the costly defense of another trial, when the jury was unable to reach a verdict on 13 counts of bribery, perjury, and conspiracy.

Flood, making full use of his seniority, held a powerful post on the defense subcommittee of the House Appropriations Committee which he used unabashedly to help Luzerne County in the post-anthracite era. In 1958 he sponsored the Flood-Douglas bill to provide federal dollars to high unemployment areas. In 1965 he was the chief House sponsor of the Appalachia Redevelopment Act, and in 1967 was named chairman of the Labor, Health, Education and Welfare subcommittee. In addition to his major role in the construction of the Wilkes-Barre Veterans Hospital, he secured federal grants worth millions of dollars for post offices and other federal facilities in his district, and was critical to the passage of the Coal Mine Health and Safety Act of 1969, the black lung legislation which benefitted former miners and their widows. Flood's courage and strength during the Agnes Disaster of 1972 became the stuff of legend, and he managed to funnel hundreds of millions of dollars in federal relief money into the area to speed its recovery.

Flood was a colorful and legendary figure. His formal cape and top hat, his white Cadillac convertible—stories of Flood abound. Even more important than the legend is the fact that Dan Flood was deeply loved by his constituents of both parties and all ethnic and racial groups. Married for 44 years to Catherine Swank, Flood died at age 90 on May 28, 1994. He received an unprecedented service in the rotunda of the Luzerne County Court House—where a grateful county bid him goodbye—and thanks.

major rebuilding incentive for businesses and homeowners alike.

With the massive infusion of government aid, Wyoming Valley came back stronger than ever from the devastation of Tropical Storm Agnes. Most residents and many businesses were able to rebuild, and in many ways the flood provided the financing necessary for Wyoming Valley to throw off the depressed remains of the anthracite era. The assets generated by flood recovery and a subsequently revitalized Wilkes-Barre were dispersed throughout Wyoming Valley and its suburbs. The people of the region, through cooperation and compassion, rebuilt their communities. Although much was lost because of the disaster, much was also gained.

Despite the success of the recovery, the flood raised some serious questions about the county's ability to deal with disaster. Studies by documentary film-maker and historian Anthony Mussari showed that Wyoming Valley was unprepared for such a calamity and that recovery work was often disorganized and inefficient. Also bickering over realms of control and questionable allocations of funding occurred in both the private and public sector. Although such problems can be expected after a major disaster, there are those who believe that the valley's resurgence could have been even greater.

Congressman Flood, the hero of the region's recovery, also came under increasing criticism. As early as 1970, questions regarding the Congressman's fund-raising methods were common among Washington insiders. The FBI and the Justice Department opened investigations in 1977. An indictment was issued which accused Flood of conspiring to solicit campaign contributions from individuals seeking government contracts. Flood was said to have received over $50,000 in cash along with one hundred shares of First Valley Bank stock. Forced to resign in 1978, he received a one year probation for his crime. Flood maintained his innocence, but agreed to plead guilty to conspiracy in order to avoid trial. At this time he was in precarious health. His supporters were forgiving despite the issue of guilt or innocence. His detractors claimed that the charge was part of a longstanding pattern of questionable politics areawide.

The flood of 1972 had a major impact upon the county's social history. The population shift to the suburbs, which started in the 1950s, was hastened considerably. Although many people wanted to remain within the county, there was an increasing desire to move from the flood plain. As a result the Back Mountain and Mountaintop witnessed a population explosion. Between 1970 and 1980 the Back Mountain grew from 24,242 residents to 30,481, while Mountaintop saw an increase from 10,035 to 14,180. Simultaneously, the flood plain municipalities of Wilkes-Barre, Kingston, and Plymouth saw population declines from 58,856 to 51,551, 18,325 to 15,681 and 9,536 to 7,605 respectively.

Suburbanization was not just a by-product of the flood. Although a leveling off of suburban populations occurred between 1980 and 1990, many valley communities continued to experience a decrease. Wilkes-Barre dropped to 45,081 residents in the 1990 census. The Hazleton area saw a similar, if not as spontaneous,

New suburban tract housing encroaching on existing farmlands in the Back Mountain following the 1972 flood.

trend. As the population of Hazleton city fell from 30,426 in 1970 to 27,318 in 1980, the number of residents in the suburbs expanded during the same decade from 15,293 to 20,476. As with Wyoming Valley, Hazleton area suburbs leveled-off during the 1980s, while the city of Hazleton fell to 24,428 residents in the 1990 count.

Suburban housing in the Berwick area.

Suburbanization occurred in the Berwick area as well. Berwick itself is in Columbia County, but its suburbs and school district include four municipalities in Luzerne County. With the construction of the Pennsylvania Power and Light (PP&L) nuclear power plant in Salem Township, the towns in this lower Susquehanna region also saw growth, expanding from 7,158 in 1970 to 8,276 in 1980.

Both the newly developed areas and the former coal towns were affected by suburbanization. There were ninety-one major demographic shifts in the outlying regions of the county. By the 1980s the area's employment pattern was shifting from agricultural and blue collar to increasingly professional. New housing developments were no longer just for those in the middle income level, but were often geared as well toward families in higher financial strata. Such high priced housing was especially noticeable in the Back Mountain, with the Sutton Hills and Bulford Farms developments. The wealth that was brought into these suburbs increased the tax base of their municipalities and school districts, and allowed for an increase in public services. Also, many older businesses expanded while a host of new establishments opened. For example, in 1960 there were only three pizza shops in the Back Mountain. By 1990 there were fourteen!

The growth of the suburbs brought negatives along with the positives. Route 309, a major traffic artery in the Back Mountain and Mountaintop, struggled to keep pace with the growth. Drinking water pollution and water shortages were a problem in a number of Back Mountain developments, while malfunctioning sewage disposal systems plagued Mountaintop. Many longtime residents feared the effects of overdevelopment, and there was concern that the influx of new residents, who often worked in Wyoming Valley or Hazleton, was creating bedroom suburbs without a real sense of community.

Suburbanization's impact was felt in the former coal towns as well. As people moved to the outlying regions,

The former Dallas High School now houses the Back Mountain Library.

the urban areas saw a drop in their tax base. As a result, cutbacks occurred in some municipal and educational services. The demographic profile of the former coal towns increased in age and dropped in income. By 1990 the percentage of Luzerne County residents over sixty-five years of age was 19.7. Only counties with large retirement communities in America's Sunbelt exceeded this figure. With more residents relying on Social Security and having limited financial resources, paying for public service programs became increasingly burdensome. In Wilkes-Barre, this created a dilemma for Mayor Lee Namey in 1993, as he faced the no-win situation of either cutting public services or raising taxes.

Other changes also affected life in Luzerne County. In Chapter Four it was noted that during the 1920s people began to identify more with their communities than with their ethnic groups. As the anthracite industry declined, community allegiance increased, as in Plymouth where residents proudly proclaimed their town motto, "Shawnee Against the World." Often this local pride was centered around the municipal high schools and their athletic teams.

This localism received a blow during the 1960s with school consolidation. The movement started in the rural and suburban areas with such jointures as Lake Lehman, Dallas Area, and Northwest Area. Then in 1963, General Assembly Act 299 was passed. By July 1, 1964, each county education board was required to establish school districts to meet the approval of the State Board of Education.

In Luzerne County this translated into a mandate for consolidation. On April 27, 1964, the county board submitted a plan calling for ten "units," replacing the sixty school districts which then existed. The three previously mentioned rural consolidations were left intact. For units such as the Greater Nanticoke Area and the Pittston Area, the presence of a central city and district-wide socioeconomic characteristics overcame the initial opposition. In Wyoming Area there was some controversy over the name since West Pittston and Exeter had populations larger than Wyoming's. The eventual agreement centered upon the belief that "Wyoming" would have more name recognition.

However, controversy raged in Units 6, 7, 9, and 10. Units 6 and 7 were eventually combined to form the Wyoming Valley West School District. The wide range of socioeconomic characteristics of these nine West Side communities—Plymouth, Larksville, Edwardsville, Kingston, Courtdale, Pringle, Luzerne, Forty Fort, and Swoyersville—along with their intense local rivalries, generated conflict within the district from the very beginning. The district's large enrollment was rather frightening to students and parents alike. In the early years of the school, graduating classes numbered well over five-hundred, a far cry from the small classes in the seven former high schools. Local sport fans dubbed Wyoming Valley West, "the monster," because of the large pool of athletes available on the West Side. Although the school district has been successful in expanding educational opportunities for its students, the merger has been accepted very reluctantly. Many believe that the school's size has impersonalized

Dallas Senior High School, 1994.

Wyoming Area Senior High School in Exeter, 1994.

think that localism in its politics has impeded large-scale educational and athletic achievement.

Opposition to Unit 9 was so strong that it never became a reality. The massive district that was proposed extended from Laflin, through Wilkes-Barre City and Hanover Township, to White Haven and Dorrance Township in the south. Residents of Plains Township, Hanover Township, and Mountaintop were most vocal in their resistance. While Plains was absorbed into the Wilkes-Barre School District, the creation of the Hanover Area School District and the Crestwood School District precluded the formation of a complete Unit 9. And within Wilkes-Barre City, local interests have succeeded in preserving three high schools, while larger Pennsylvania cities such as Scranton and Harrisburg have only one public academic high school.

From its inception in 1964 until 1992, three public high schools continued to function in Unit 10. Hazleton, West Hazleton and Freeland all retained their separate identities under the auspices of the Hazleton Area School District, the largest district in the county. Local pride and the absence of a single high school to house all the students were the major obstacles. The opposition was so strong in the suburban Conyngham Valley that the area made an unsuccessful attempt to secede from the district. With the completion of a new building in Hazle Township in 1992, classes commenced in the newly consolidated Hazleton Area High School. Despite some confusion in the first weeks and sentimental longings for the old schools, the new high school was generally praised. Considering the interest in local high school sports, the success of the Cougars' basketball team helped make the merger more palatable.

Crestwood High School in Mountaintop, 1994.

While the advocates of school consolidation achieved their objectives, those who favored municipal consolidation found little success. The rationale for bringing the county's seventy-six incorporated communities under the banner of one or two large cities was compelling. Through consolidation Wyoming Valley itself could become Pennsylvania's third largest city, with a population of approximately 250,000. Public services could operate more efficiently under single control rather than

HIGHER EDUCATION IN LUZERNE COUNTY

The first baccalaureate degree granting college in Luzerne County was College Misericordia in Dallas. Founded in 1924 by the Roman Catholic Sisters of Mercy, its mission was to educate young women. Misericordia graduates entered elementary and secondary teaching, home economics, fine arts, and nursing. Men have been admitted as full time students since the late 1980s. Misericordia now places a strong emphasis on health care professions in both undergraduate and graduate programs, and has accomplished a large scale building program for student housing and athletic facilities. Today, Misericordia serves over 1,500 students on its Back Mountain campus.

Wilkes University was founded as Bucknell Junior College in 1933. Open to both men and women, in 1947 it became Wilkes College, a four-year, independent, non-denominational, liberal arts and pre-professional institution. Wilkes expanded its faculty, research facilities, and community service activities, and in 1990, became Wilkes University. The school is now the home of over 2,000 undergraduates with an additional 600 graduate students. Many of the most beautiful homes in Wilkes-Barre's Historic Preservation District were donated to the school for use as college facilities.

A group of Holy Cross Fathers from the University of Notre Dame responded to the invitation of Scranton Diocese Bishop William J. Hafey to organize King's College in 1946. Returning veterans, taking advantage of the G.I. Bill, constituted all of the first graduating class in 1950. The school occupies a modern campus in north central Wilkes-Barre, just two blocks from the south central campus of Wilkes. Coeducational since 1970, the 1980s witnessed an increasing number of out-of-town students, and the 1990s brought a commitment to graduate education with programs in the William G. McGowan School of Business and the College of Arts and Sciences. Today King's enrolls over 1,700 full-time students along with 600 part-time students.

With nearly 4,000 full and part-time students, Luzerne County Community College is the county's largest college. In 1965 the County Commissioners agreed to sponsor a two-year community college for residents. The first class of 210 graduated from the temporary Wilkes-Barre campus in 1969. In 1974 LCCC moved to its 122 acre campus in Nanticoke. The school provides the first two years of general education, and in addition, offers preparation for careers in nursing, other health care specialties, and a wide range of technical fields. Luzerne County Community College has graduated nearly 12,000 students and provided professional training, vocational instruction, and personal enrichment courses for thousands more.

Requested by Wilkes-Barre's Chamber of Commerce and Rotary Club, the Pennsylvania State University instituted the first program of higher education in Luzerne County in 1916 to provide advanced technology courses. After World War II it expanded to meet increased demand, and in 1968, moved to the former estate of the John Conyngham family, a 50 acre site in Lehman Township. Since that time the school has expanded its physical plant and academic curriculum. The school offers associate degrees and a limited number of baccalaureate degrees in technological fields. Entry to the Main or Capitol campuses following the first two years of study at Penn State Wilkes-Barre draws many students interested in the applied sciences. Currently, over 1,000 students are enrolled.

Pennsylvania State University at Hazleton is geared toward business and general education. It first opened its doors in 1934 for 47 students at the downtown Hazleton Markle Bank Building. In 1948 Penn State Hazleton moved to the 80 acre Markle Estate in West Hazleton. Dormitories now house 485 students there. The Hazleton campus has kept its strong commitment to a two-year general education program, although associate degree programs in technological fields, business, and physical therapy assistant have recently become popular. Nearly ninety percent of the students eventually work toward their baccalaureate degree. At present, 1,200 students attend Penn State Hazleton.

Many of the graduates of these local colleges have left the area, but those who have remained have formed a professional and technological nucleus in Luzerne County. Without its colleges and universities, each with its own distinct character, the region's dreams of economic revitalization would have been dashed.

The entry gate and chapel in front of College Misericordia in Dallas, Pa.

SPEV, a costumed ensemble which performs Slovak folk music, is part of the Slovak Heritage Society of Northeastern PA. The Society was founded in 1984 to advance the awareness of Slovak heritage and culture among all people.

being dispersed throughout the county, and might even bring about a decrease in taxes. However, these arguments fell on deaf ears.

Opponents questioned the projections, and the problems encountered by large city governments were cited as evidence to thwart consolidation. Local political bosses fought the movement in order to retain control over the patronage system. Others presented the case that consolidation would take government away from the people. The combined voices of opposition effectively ended the consolidation movement. The number of municipalities in the county actually grew during this period with the formation of new boroughs at Harveys Lake, Penn Lake Park, and Bear Creek Village.

The advocates of consolidation did, and still do, have some strong arguments, especially in light of the financial difficulties faced by Wilkes-Barre, Kingston, and Forty Fort in 1993. However, they failed to understand the mood of the people. With the demise of the local high schools and the questions regarding the new jointures, county residents were reluctant to lose their remaining community identity. In an area which prefers stability over change, transformation was simply occurring too rapidly.

The role of ethnicity was also undergoing change in Luzerne County. In 1960, it was not uncommon to hear such languages as Polish and Italian spoken throughout the county. Most ethnic churches scheduled at least one Sunday Mass in their native tongue while conversation at local business establishments still included the language of the dominant immigrant group. By 1990, however, there were few immigrants from eastern or southern Europe left, and children of these immigrants relied almost exclusively upon English. Although foreign language classes are offered at local schools, they are taken for general interest rather than from necessity.

The ethnic enclaves are not in evidence to the extent to which they once were. Migration out of the county, intermarriage between people of different ethnic and religious backgrounds, and changing attitudes have made most neighborhoods culturally mixed. It is simply more practical for the current residents of the county to focus their lives on family and community rather than on ethnic heritage.

Despite the lessening ethnic ties, visitors to the region often remark that the bonds to the old world cultures are remarkably strong. While ethnic culture may not be the dominant force that it once was, county residents emphasize their roots to a greater degree than most Americans. The reason for this is somewhat complex, but nevertheless quite important in understanding the area.

The social and economic interlocking of people within each ethnic group is one way in which these communities can support individuals within them. One example is ethnic community support for a particular business owned by a member of that community. The business may or may not provide a culturally specific need for the community. If it does, there is extra motivation for the community's support. But even if there is no special ethnic overtone to the business, where one member of a community succeeds, that person is in a position to help others along.

Interactive support for one's ethnic community often means support for specific churches and schools. There is always the danger that without the ethnic community's backing, the wherewithal to keep that church or school going will not be available, and an important part of family and community tradition will be lost.

Throughout much of the county's past, residents clung to their cultural groups as a form of social insurance that buffered their dealings with the rigid employment and social structure of the mining industry, where most operations were ultimately owned by one of the giant railroad corporations. Personalizing that huge corporate structure meant finding some kind of connecting link to someone within it. To be of a specific ethnic group usually went a long way in helping to create the social, political, and economic links that determined one's job and social status.

People identified with their particular ethnic group not only for reasons of cultural familiarity, but also because they had numerous social and economic ties to that group. As a result, not only did ethnic cohesion develop but so too did social and economic solidarity. Since the coal culture is only one generation removed from the present day, many county residents over thirty can identify with this phenomenon, and ethnic identification and pride are still strong. In areas in the county and northeastern Pennsylvania where the coal industry continued to dominate beyond the 1960s, the tendency to identify with the ethnic culture continues to be a major influence.

This degree of ethnic identification is demonstrated by the more than 150 ethnic churches that still operate in Luzerne County. While their native tongue is used only occasionally, the ethnic culture continues to be honored through church festivals, bazaars, musical productions, and traditional ceremonies. In fact, on any weekend in the summer, there is at least one church sponsored bazaar featuring special ethnic foods and music.

In politics there is a conscious effort to balance the ticket from an ethnic perspective, and most people in the county are very aware of their cultural heritage, and knowledgeable about it. Special traditions are still observed, especially during the holidays, as the grandchildren and great-grandchildren of the immigrants continue to pass their customs on to their offspring.

The modern era has witnessed additional change in the ethnic composition of Luzerne County. Although the influx of new arrivals is not as massive as at the turn of the century, there is a marked increase in the number of African Americans, Hispanics, and Asians. The minority population in Luzerne County has risen from 4,700 in 1980 to 8,128 in 1990. During this decade the number of African American residents grew from 2,101 to 4,013, Hispanics from 1,365 to 1,834, and Asians from 855 to 1,355. New ethnic communities, such as the Hispanics in Hazleton and the Vietnamese in Wilkes-Barre, have developed in recent years.

As in the past, immigration to

The Pittston Tomato Festival has grown from a handful of vendors to a major area event. Judy Strelish pins sash on Miss Tomato 1991, Kira Jugus, as Maria Olivieri, Miss Tomato 1990, looks on.

Hispanic members of St. Gabriel's Church, Hazleton, performing a traditional dance at a Latin American party in the church hall in 1992.

Dedication of the "Celebrating Our Diversity" mural on the corner of South and South Main Streets, Wilkes-Barre. The Mural was conceived and painted by members of the Interfaith Resource Center for Peace and Justice and its Dismantling Racism Committee.

The closing for the Earth Conservancy, in October 1994, was attended by: (seated from left to right) Eugene Roth, Michael A. Dziak, Christopher N. Breiseth, (standing) James G. O'Karma, Frank J. McDonnell, R. Denny Schmidt, James S. Hays, Steven P. Roth, and Mark A. Van Loon.

Luzerne County has not always been easy for the newcomers. Discrimination and resentment are often evident, and there are complaints that the new arrivals take jobs away from long-time residents. This assertion is unfounded, however, since studies have shown that migrants often take the jobs not wanted by more established citizens. Plus, the number of recent arrivals is not large enough to effect any displacement of workers.

Unfortunately, during poor economic times people often look for scapegoats. While hate crimes are not the norm in Luzerne County, acts of violence and intolerance have occurred throughout the region. In July 1992, racial tensions in Wilkes-Barre's East End broke into a street fight. The following year racist graffiti was spray painted throughout a south Wilkes-Barre playground. Often discrimination is more subtle. Suspicion and misconceptions regarding African Americans and Hispanics are sometimes expressed even by otherwise well-meaning county residents. Luzerne County citizens, whose ancestors were once the victims of discrimination, have sometimes become the perpetrators of prejudice themselves.

The new arrivals also face poverty, as did the newcomers of the preceeding century. While only 10.8 percent of the county's white citizens live below the poverty line, the figure is 45.9 percent for African Americans, 33.3 percent for Hispanics, and 18.8 percent for Asians. For Native Americans it is 15.4 percent. Minorities hold few positions in the public sector while only a handful of upper level private sector jobs go to non-whites.

The 1980s and 1990s have brought economic and social progress to Luzerne County. In Wyoming Valley, the rebuilding since the 1972 flood has resulted in a modern, urban landscape of considerable character and aesthetic interest, thanks to the architectural masterpieces surviving from its era of greatest prosperity. Businesses continue to grow on the outskirts of Wilkes-Barre and Hazleton, while affluent developments dot the suburbs.

The Earth Conservancy, organized under the aegis of Congressman Paul Kanjorski, is working on the development of 16,000 acres of former coal land. The project is focused on the technological challenge of cleaning up an environment—both land and water—damaged during a century of mining, with the goal of creating a variety of high-tech jobs in the process. The immediate benefits include the repayment of eight million dollars in back taxes owed by the Blue Coal

Company to the county and its municipalities and school districts. The long term development of this undertaking has brought the promise of future growth through the studied utilization of land resources.

Problems still exist within the county. Unemployment, underemployment, and outright poverty are found in the most affluent municipalities. Misunderstanding of the new arrivals to the region has brought increasing social tension. And with the growth of suburban malls and shopping centers, maintaining the downtown business districts of Wilkes-Barre, Hazleton, Pittston, and Nanticoke has become challenging.

As we move toward the 21th century, there is hope for a bright future in Luzerne County. Although the economic base of the region is changing once again, many signs indicate continued growth and development. The managed community expansion and the reclamation of land devastated by the coal era have created many attractive settings in both rural and urban areas throughout the county. As in the past, however, the real strength of Luzerne County is its people. Their diversity has been the hallmark of its history, and their common goals for the region will be the source of unity for its future.

Rehabilitation of the Pomeroy's building, downtown Wilkes-Barre began in 1993.

Partners in Progress

Luzerne County is one of Pennsylvania's most diverse regions economically, culturally, politically, and historically. Its constant struggle amongst opposing factions and natural disasters, along with economic hard times has strengthened the community's ability to be poised for the future. The people of Luzerne County have moved together to form positive business and educational leadership that will serve the region well for years to come.

Wyoming Historical and Geological Society

The Wyoming Historical and Geological Society was founded in 1858 on the 50th anniversary of the first burning of anthracite coal in an open grate by Judge Jesse Fell. The thought of those gathered at the tavern was "that there are still preserved in our midst many memorials, papers, records, and relics of local and general historical interest which...if gathered up, would form a collection of increasing interest and value."

Throughout its 136 year history, the Society has maintained its mission to collect, preserve, and interpret the history, geology, genealogy, architecture and archeology of Luzerne County, and to educate its citizens to their heritage.

The Society museum, located behind the Osterhout Free Library on South Franklin Street in Wilkes-Barre, contains three floors of exhibits that interpret the history of the anthracite coal industry and the life-style of the early Native American inhabitants of northeastern Pennsylvania. These two permanent displays are augmented by changing exhibits which illustrate specific events in local history. The Society also sponsors special lectures, educational programs and tours which are open to the public. The museum is open Tuesday through Saturday.

A short distance from the museum, at 49 South Franklin Street, is the Bishop Memorial Library, which houses more than 6,000 bound volumes of local history, in addition to newspapers, manuscript collections, photographs, and maps covering the entire chronology of Luzerne County. Its research facilities are available Tuesday through Saturday for the serious scholar as well as for the avocational historian.

Swetland Homestead, at 885 Wyoming Avenue, Wyoming, is the Society's historic house museum. The Homestead, listed on the National Register of Historic Places, includes the settlers' cabin built in 1797 by Connecticut farmer Luke Swetland. The additions to the house through 1860 reflect the changes which took place as America and Wyoming Valley passed from an agrarian economy to an industrialized society. Annual events include a Revolutionary War Encampment and reenactment of the 1778 Battle of Wyoming in July and candlelight tours each December.

The wealth of bibliographic material in the Society's collection has been incorporated into numerous publications. The records of the original Connecticut settlers form the basis of *The Susquehannah Company Papers*, an 11-volume set, which has received national acclaim. *The Whole Valley Cookbook, African-Americans in the Wyoming Valley* and *Ghost Towns of North Mountain* have also received state and national recognition.

Other publishing endeavors of the Society include *Wilkes-Barre Architecture 1860-1960, Steamboats on the Susquehanna, Bridging Change: A Wyoming Valley Sketchbook, Harvey's Lake,* and *Luzerne County: History of the People and Culture.*

Historic Swetland Homestead.

The Society Museum, built in 1893.

The Bishop Memorial Library.

Motor Twins

Russell Frantz is shown during the introduction of the first post-war Ford. Next to Mr. Frantz is his wife.

Founded in 1920 by Russell Frantz 12 years after the Ford Motor Company produced its first Model T automobile, Motor Twins has become one of the preeminent car dealerships in Luzerne County.

Mr. Frantz continued as president until 1964 when his son, Charles Frantz took over running the company. Charles Frantz continued the business until 1985 when Steve Morenko purchased the company.

Russell Frantz began his business in Wilkes-Barre and later opened a showroom in Kingston. The two locations have been in continuous business, braving the floods of 1936, 1940 and the Agnes Flood of 1972 when the Susquehanna River crested at 45 feet flooding the valley. All of the inventory in the Kingston building was saved but the Wilkes-Barre location was a total loss. With the help of loyal employees the dealership reopened in 10 days for business as usual.

Mr. Morenko began working for Motor Twins in 1952 when he was 24 years old. When asked the future of Motor Twins and the American car industry, Mr. Morenko replied "...that the American companies have relearned how to make quality cars and now the cars are on an average as good as the Japanese cars and in some cases surpass them in quality."

A lineup of 1940 Ford trucks.

In 1949 white walls were the rage. A post-war Ford is shown in the Wilkes-Barre location.

The Citizens' Voice

The Citizens' Voice building.

The Citizens' Voice was born of a labor dispute and, over 16 years, has become a newspaper of the community, by the community and for the community.

The Voice's first edition was published October 9, 1978. A few days earlier, 205 employees of the Wilkes-Barre Publishing Company had gone on strike against that company.

Over the years, The Citizens' Voice has evolved into an employee-owned newspaper that continues the tradition of community-based journalism.

From neighborhood issues such as drug-free school zones, to state issues such as historic preservation, to national issues including trade, health care reform and the election of our leaders, The Citizens' Voice has fostered positions that seek to enhance the quality of life and the economic growth of the region.

For many years running, The Citizens' Voice has received awards from local and state professional organizations.

The Voice's very name embodies its principles: To be a forum, a friend and a business partner of the community.

The first "home" for the Voice was rented space in a building scheduled for demolition by the Redevelopment Authority on North Main Street, Wilkes-Barre. The newspaper leased press time from a small weekly paper.

Early in 1979, The Voice moved to rented quarters on the mezzanine of the Hotel Sterling and, also that year, a larger press was leased and placed in a production facility in Plymouth.

Consolidation of all operations occurred in June 1984 when the Voice moved into the former Boston Store warehouse on North Washington Street. A larger press and state-of-the-art computer equipment were installed.

The Citizens' Voice, Inc., was established in February 1989, officially ending the labor dispute and launching The Citizens' Voice into the realm of employee-owned publications.

The Voice's board of directors includes representatives from the business community, thereby strengthening its position in a competitive market.

In May 1993, The Citizens' Voice launched The Sunday Voice, moving into seven-day competition with the city's other daily and Sunday newspaper. The Voice's Sunday venture followed the demise of the 87-year-old Sunday Independent.

The Citizens' Voice/Sunday Voice has a tradition of a strong news report centered on the initiative of its reporters and editors. Its news and sports pages cover the spectrum of happenings in the community.

Extensive space is devoted on the editorial and op-ed pages to letters and commentary from citizens. The Citizens' Voice is the forum of the community.

The Citizens' Voice/Sunday Voice staff includes people with years of experience in the industry. These people, most of whom have roots in the community, offer the personal touch so often missing at revolving-door newspaper operations.

As newspaper technology advances, the Voice will continue to progress and produce a quality newspaper well into the 21st Century.

The Citizens' Voice/Sunday Voice family looks forward to being a part of the continuing growth of the Greater Wyoming Valley as its people remain committed to the principles that truly make it the Voice of the community.

College Misericordia

The first college, the first to offer Master's degrees in Luzerne County, College Misericordia has been in the forefront of education since its founding on September 24, 1924.

The college was the dream of the Religious Sisters of Mercy to build a Motherhouse and a college to provide a quality liberal arts education for the young women of the area.

In 1913 the order purchased 100 acres on a hilltop in Dallas. But it was eleven years before the Administration Building was constructed and the first class of 37 students entered.

From that beginning Misericordia has grown to a co-educational college with 1,800 students and 84 full-time faculty, with a 14:1 faculty/student ratio. Currently the college is graduating more than 300 students each year in associate, bachelor's and master's degrees.

In the last 10 years the college has grown substantially, building 16 townhouses for student residences, a $5.5 million Anderson Sports-Health Center, a $3.5 million residence hall and the Anderson Athletic Fields complex.

Most notable is the Alternative Learner's Project which enables learning disabled students to successfully complete college degrees and move into professional careers, as well as the continuing education program which includes an accelerated degree and second bachelor's degree programs.

While preparing its students to take their place in the society, Misericordia has provided the Campus Ministry as one of the instruments to accomplish a wide variety of community service. Under this program the students can offer their services as volunteers at local soup kitchens, adopt local senior citizens, organize children's parties, work with underprivileged local youth and help the poor in Appalachia and the South Bronx.

Extensive cultural events are available to the community including the "Theater-On-The-Green" program which presents professional Shakespearean theatre and a Shakespeare for Children program each summer.

The college holds an annual "Institute of Sacred Scripture" in which religious scholars of all faiths meet to discuss their research, current trends and issues.

A chemistry class c. 1930.

Misericordia has become the headquarters for the Ethics Institute of Northeast Pennsylvania, the Aging Religious Institute, the Institute of Law and Religious Life, and the Diversity Institute.

But growth and diversity has not diminished the mission of its founding.

What makes College Misericordia education distinct is the mission which instills in young people a commitment to Judeo-Christian values and community service. The focus is on students. Misericordia helps them develop by living the mission with them until it becomes a part of how to live.

A trio of students studying in the college library.

Luzerne County Community College

Luzerne County Community College's first site at 19-21 North River Street, Wilkes-Barre.

Luzerne County Community College became a reality on December 15, 1965 when the Luzerne County Commissioners adopted a resolution agreeing to act as sponsor of a two-year college under the Pennsylvania "Community College Act of 1963."

The commissioners appointed the County Board of School Directors to survey the needs of high school students and local employers. On September 15, 1966 the Pennsylvania State Board of Education, on information presented by the commissioners, approved the plan for the college.

The college formally began operations on October 2, 1967 when approximately 630 full-time and 200 part-time students began attending classes in temporary quarters in Wilkes-Barre.

By the Fall of 1968, enrollment totaled 1,500 and in June 1969, the first 210 students graduated.

In January 1974, the college moved to its permanent 122 acre campus in Nanticoke. The college continues to grow and now includes 12 academic buildings while employing more than 750 individuals. Enrollment in the Fall of 1993 grew to 7,450 full and part-time credit students and 8,000 full and part-time credit-free students.

A variety of educational programs and support services are offered to provide opportunities for persons to pursue an education consistent with their interests, capabilities and employment demands.

In addition to classes on the main campus, the college has 16 off-campus extension sites in six surrounding counties offering 16 two-year Liberal Arts and Science programs, 38 two-year technical career programs and 27 programs which lead to a one-year certificate of specialization.

With the addition of an $8 million Advanced Technology Center in 1988, the college offers an array of high-technology programs such as robotics and laser-electro optics. The Center also serves as a training and retraining center for Northeastern Pennsylvania businesses and offers comprehensive teleconference facilities, computer workstations and training laboratories, as well as seminar and meeting rooms.

The college has earned full accreditation by the Middle States Association of Colleges and Schools, the American Dental Association and the National League of Nursing. Cooperative agreements have been established with 23 community agencies, while articulation agreements have been established with 21 baccalaureate colleges and universities.

Today, the college boasts more than 12,500 degree-bearing alumni, and has embarked upon a 35 million dollar campus construction and renovation project aimed at positioning the college for its next several decades of service to the community.

Today at Nanticoke there are 12 modern buildings.

Diamond Manufacturing Company

Diamond Manufacturing Company is the story of two men and a woman who refused to admit failure and through their entrepreneurial spirit built an organization upon the ashes of the Exeter Machine Shops.

It is the story of John N. Thomas who founded the firm in 1915, Nellie Corcoran and William M. Powell, son-in-law of Thomas, under whose management the business grew and prospered until today it has become the nation's technological leader in the perforation of steel and other material.

During the operation of Exeter Company, Thomas opened a small perforating plant in hopes of entering the field of perforated screen used in the mines to size coal. Named Diamond Manufacturing Company, it survived the demise of Exeter and was moved to the present site in Wyoming, PA.

William Powell took over the company in 1923 after the death of Thomas. During his tenure, he improved the financial base and put Diamond on solid financial footing. He was responsible for making Diamond a factor in the perforating industry until his death in1951. At this time David C. Hall, husband of Powell's daughter Marian, became President and guided the company in the direction of industrial usage of perforated metal until he left in 1959 at which time Frank Foster stepped in to manage the firm for three years.

Charles D. Flack, husband of Joan Powell, Powell's other daughter, took over the Presidency in 1962 and steered Diamond through the 60s and 70s making massive equipment changes and seeking new markets that were opening in the American economy. He led the firm into aircraft, appliance, air and water pollution control and the growing field of noise and acoustical controls. Working with perforating machine manufacturers in Germany, Flack assisted in the development of a new generation computerized perforating press.

With Flack's death in 1979, the Presidency passed to his son, Charles Jr. Educated at Susquehanna, he continued the pursuit of industrial markets using high technology machinery and tooling as well as pursuing the highest quality standards in the industry. He and his brother Harold, J. N. Thomas' great grandsons, own and operate what is now the largest perforating company in North America with plants in Wyoming, PA as well as in Maryland and Indiana.

An incubator with newborn chicks.

Two of the computerized presses used by Diamond Manufacturing in process of metal perforation.

Wyoming Seminary

Wyoming

REESE, ROBERT MORRIS
Kingston, Pa.
"Bob"
Entered 1923, College Preparatory, Amphictyon, Opinator Board (5), Annual Board (5), Second Honors (3) (4).
"He that respects himself is safe from others;
He wears a coat of mail that none can pierce."

REYNOLDS, GEORGE J.
Wilkes-Barre, Pa.
Trucksville, Pa.
Entered 1922, College Preparatory, Independent, Class President (2), Honor Student (2), Second Vice-President of Class (3), Assistant Business Manager of Opinator (3) (4), Assistant Cheer Leader (4), Vice-President of Society (4), Corresponding Secretary of Society (4), Assistant Business Manager of Dramatics (4), Handbook Board (4), President of Class (5), Vice-President of Y. M. C. A. (5), Y. M. C. A. Council (5), Business Manager of Opinator (5), Business Manager of Dramatics (5), President Society (5).
"Nature might stand up and say to all the world, 'This is a man.'"

TODD, MADOLIN,
Oneonta, N. Y.
"Toddie"
Entered 1924, Literary Scientific, Plattonian, Vice-President of Girls' Student Council (4), President Society (5), Ring Committee (5), Glee Club (5).
"Good sense and good nature are never separated."

Early 20th century graduates were featured in the Wyoming *yearbook.*

In September 1844, in the rural village of Kingston, 14 girls and 17 boys became the first Wyoming Seminary students. The new school stood among orchards and farm fields and became one of America's first coeducational boarding schools.

Seminary's first students came from towns and villages throughout Pennsylvania and New York.

Students sought "an education that will fit them for every useful employment in life; to cultivate the soil, conduct the mechanical, mercantile or commercial interests of the country, and guard with the integrity of a Washington the liberties of the nation," as the school's founders stated in 1844.

In the 1850's, students arrived by four-horse coach, by canal boat, or by raft. After two weeks of boarding with a Kingston spinster, Benjamin Hall walked 25 miles home to Tunkhannock – for a good meal. "I had spent two weeks of my life without eating too much," he later wrote.

The school grew its own produce and raised livestock. A smoke house preserved meat for the winter, while spices, coffee, tea, and sugar were hauled from Philadelphia by canal boat. In the dining room, "the girls sat in unbroken rows next to the wall, while in similar unbroken rows across the table sat the young men."

"I think they are very strict here: students have to get up at five in the morning and study an hour and a half before breakfast and study from seven until half after nine in the evening and they must be in bed at ten o'clock when the bell rings," wrote a student in the 1850's.

The nation's new industrial age brought growth to the Wyoming Valley. Railroad and steel industries needed the Valley's anthracite coal, and train service came to Kingston in 1856, bringing industrial life to the doorstep of campus. The apple orchard had vanished. The fields and forests had become new streets with shops, industries and homes.

The school grew significantly, adding a business school to prepare students for the region's mining, banking and manufacturing concerns. The college preparatory program readied young men and women for success at leading colleges and new universities.

Athletic competitions became increasingly popular after the Civil War. Seminary boys took up the national pastime of baseball, while tennis, archery and croquet provided outdoor exercise for girls. In 1892, the Wyoming Seminary football team made history, participating in the world's first night football game in Mansfield, Pa.

For many young men, athletics were more than a pleasant diversion providing an opportunity for education. Dr. Levi Sprague, the president of Wyoming Seminary for 54 years, would routinely tour anthracite mining towns, searching for promising young men and women. He found them among the breaker boys and the young women in domestic service.

Other students helped pay the tuition by tending the boiler, running the electric light plant, and ringing the daily bells.

Class rolls of the period show an ethnically diverse student body, as the early 20th century brought European immigrants to the Wyoming Valley, seeking work for themselves and education for their children.

As American education changed, so did the school's mission. A 1951 merger with the Wilkes-Barre Day School made Wyoming Seminary the region's only independent school to offer a complete program from nursery school through secondary school. The business and music schools were dissolved in the mid-1960s.

The 1960s were tempestuous times for campuses throughout the country. At Wyoming Seminary, social change was combined with physical change.

When Hurricane Agnes devastated the area in June 1972, more than five feet of water washed over the campus. Miraculously, school opened only a week late in September. Books, desks, and other equipment were lost, but under the leadership of President Wallace F. Stettler, the school emerged a stronger institution.

New buildings, including a 460-seat performing arts center, a 20,000 volume library and learning center, and a modern student activities center, were constructed in the 1970s. They complement the school's 19th century buildings which are listed on the National Register of Historic Places.

Under the leadership of President H. Jeremy Packard, Wyoming Seminary is celebrating its 150th anniversary in 1994. Today students come from not only Pennsylvania, New York, and New Jersey, but from California, Texas, and Alaska, the Caribbean, Europe and Asia. More than 700 students are enrolled from nursery through twelfth grade and the postgraduate year. Small classes, close ties among faculty and students, and strong emphasis on the written and spoken word are the legacy of the school's founders.

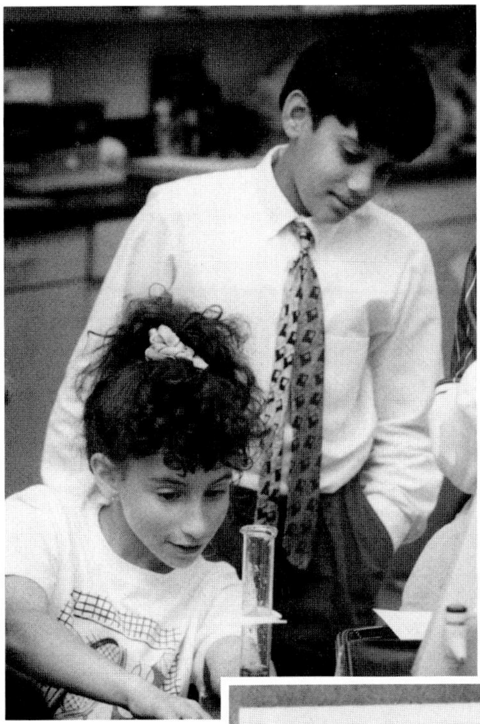

Middle school science class.

The Annual *board.*

Luzerne Products

Stuart M. Bell, President of Luzerne Products

Luzerne Products Inc. began operations in the Wyoming Valley in August 1967 by building a plant to serve the E.I. duPont organization in the processing and repacking of synthetic fibers in the northeastern United States market.

Luzerne Products is owned by James E. Bell, Hobe Sound, Florida, a former duPont executive, and managed locally by his son Stuart M. Bell.

The plant was under construction in 1967, and the first warp beams were produced in February 1968. The facility had been in continuous operation through 1986. E.I. duPont moved its operations to the south and then no longer needed the services of Luzerne Products in the northeastern United States.

At this time James E. Bell, the founder and owner of Luzerne Products Inc., was faced with a decision, whether to sell the property and sever his ties with Wyoming Valley, or attempt to find a new business that could utilize the plant's facilities. This was a difficult decision as Mr. Bell had several offers to sell the building, but he decided to lease rather than sell the building and lose touch with his business contacts in the Wilkes-Barre area.

In 1986 Luzerne Products Inc. turned from a manufacturing concern to a property management company. Currently Luzerne Products employs five full time employees who oversee and maintain the plant facilities for two tenants. The two tenants employ more than 200 individuals on a full time basis.

Luzerne also leases approximately ten acres to a local farmer who is currently growing corn on the land.

In November of 1992 James E. Bell's youngest son, Stuart M. Bell, became president of Luzerne Products. Stuart had worked for the Chase Manhattan Bank for six years and was a vice president at that bank when he decided to move to the Wilkes-Barre area and become president of the family owned business. Stuart hopes to expand the family business by finding other business and investment opportunities in the area. Over the years Luzerne Products has looked at several other businesses to purchase or invest in, but hasn't found a correct match yet.

Stuart believes that by moving to the area he will come to know the area better and this will facilitate finding a new business opportunity that Luzerne Products can expand into, allowing the business to grow into the future.

Site of operations on Courtright Street in Plains.

Hazleton-St. Joseph Medical Center

St. Joseph's Hospital, Hazleton, founded by the Bernardine Sisters of St. Francis, began operation in July 1944 as the Corrigan Maternity Hospital with Dr. John J. James and Dr. Lawrence F. Corrigan as staff physicians.

The hospital grew rapidly and in four years there were 4,400 admissions and 4,341 births were recorded.

Hazleton at that time was served by a Pennsylvania State Hospital and the need for a general hospital was felt through the region.

In December 1946 the Bernardine Sisters applied to Bishop William S. Hafey of the Scranton Diocese to begin a drive for the seed money necessary to construct a $2 million, 300 bed general hospital. Thomas Kennedy, President of the United Mine Workers Union was named diocesan vice chairman and Frank Correale, general chairman.

The drive raised $375,425 from the community's 23 parishes in the Hazleton Deanery and the Bishop's House of Charity contributed another $450,000. The first step toward the construction of St. Joseph's Hospital began on September 8, 1946 when Bishop Hafey and Mr. Correale together broke ground for the new hospital. Also present at the ceremony was Mother M. Edmund, superior general of the Bernardine Sisters of St. Francis. In November 1949, what was called the most modern hospital in eastern Pennsylvania, began full operation.

The 1950's witnessed the growth as a staff of 350 cared for more than 700,000 patients.

As the populations of the Greater Hazleton area grew, so too did St. Joseph's as it kept pace with developing technology in the field of medicine. A new intensive care facility was created and a computer system was installed.

The hospital board of trustees embarked on a massive expansion in the diagnostic surgical, radiological and other specialized areas in the health-care field.

During the 1980's the hospital responded to the need for medical service to the small communities surrounding Hazleton.

In 1981, when Pennsylvania closed the Locust Mountain State General Hospital in Shenandoah, the first satellite was established.

The satellite operations would eventually be extended to the communities of Weatherly, Conyngham, Sugarloaf, Tresckow, Ringtown, Freeland and Tamaqua. Combining its satellite system with the Ambulatory Care Center, St. Joseph's has brought to the door-step medical services that were unavailable to these communities in the past.

The hospital also operates a multi-phase Outpatient Rehabilitation Center and Fitness Center, which houses a Cancer Treatment Center run by a group of independent physicians.

To meet the growing demand for service, the hospital has constructed on its grounds a medical-arts building and has plans for the renovation of an old wing of the hospital.

Ground breaking ceremony September 8, 1946. The Rev. Mother M. Edmund, Supr. Gen., Bernardine Sisters, Mr. Frank Correale, President, Hospital Board, His Excellancy, William J. Haffey, Bishop of Scranton.

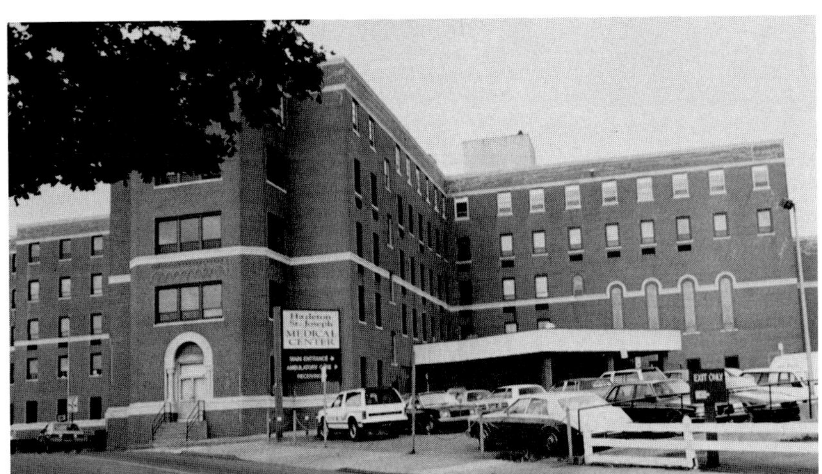

The Medical Center on Route 309, just north of downtown Hazleton.

Bedwick & Jones Printing, Inc.

Standing, Ray Bedwick, seated, Peg Jones and Bob Jones.

One of Luzerne County's oldest printing establishments, Bedwick and Jones Printing, Inc. was founded in 1961 by Robert Jones and Raymond Bedwick. The two men met while working for Planters Peanuts and shared a common dream–owning their own business. At Planters, Jones, 19 years old, was a printer and Bedwick, 21 years old, worked in sales.

With a small investment they purchased a second hand press and set up a print shop in Wilkes-Barre. Jones was responsible for production and Bedwick for soliciting the customers.

In 1964 the growth of the business necessitated a move to larger quarters in the Kingston Corners building and hiring additional production staff. After the 1972 flood, the local fire trucks hosed down the equipment, which had been completely covered with water. The business relocated to Sans Souci highway and was back in business within several weeks. In 1977 a new facility was built in the then new Hanover Industrial Park where it remains today.

Peg Jones joined the company in 1986 to expedite the further expansion of the business. An addition to the building allowed the company to enter the computer age with the purchase of several new pieces of equipment including imagesetters, presses, cutters, folders and darkroom equipment.

Although the company boasts the latest in technology, the strength of the company lies with the team of craftsmen and women who produce quality products for clients from New York and Pennsylvania. Everyone at Bedwick and Jones is a member of the Total Quality Management team and is committed to forming partnerships with vendors and customers in order to meet and exceed the customers expectations.

The firm produces single and multi-color commercial materials.

In 1986 computers were installed.

Rita DePasquale, office manager in front of present facility.

The Hazleton National Bank

In 1890, a group of businessmen in the Hazleton area centered their community-minded energies on the establishment of a financial institution. Original board members drew heavily from the flourishing coal industry of the era, and a local contractor, a doctor, and several merchants and prominent residents also helped form the Hazleton National Bank. The organization was granted its charter in January of 1890. Its first president was A.S. Van Wickle. The original site of the bank was on the south side of Broad Street between Laurel and Wyoming, the former location of The Hazleton Savings Bank.

Van Wickle and others such as Elliot P. Kisner, the "Sage of Kastanienwald," led the bank in its steady growth and expansion. Historically, the Hazleton National Bank was the forerunner of mergers and acquisitions in the area. Through careful, solid beginnings with deposits of $223,000 in July of 1890, to deposits of $1,074,000 in January of 1984, the bank acquired and established regional locations to better serve the public. The Weatherly, Lehighton, Weissport, and Nuremburg Banks all became part of the Hazleton National Bank family from the early 1940s to the late 1960s. In addition, new locations were established in Hazleton and Conyngham.

The Bank's success led to its membership in the First Valley Corporation, a Lehigh Valley based holding company. Operating under its original charter, the bank expanded its services and technology. In January of 1988, UJB Financial of Princeton, New Jersey, acquired First Valley Corporation. By 1993 the bank had assets of $466,491,000. The reorganization of UJB Financial had Hazleton and Hanover Bank of Wilkes-Barre assuming the First Valley Bank name, becoming part of the 74-office institution. It's doubtful the early founders could ever have imagined the height to which the bank has soared.

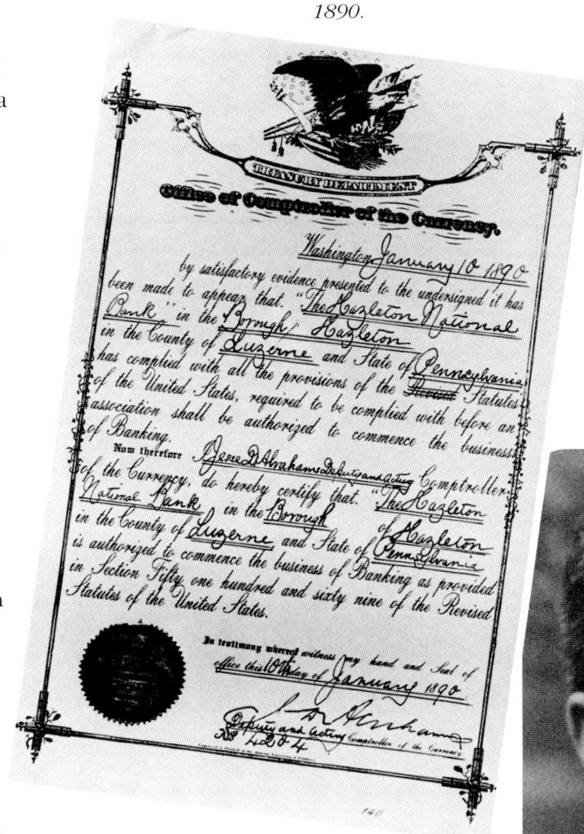

Treasury Department

Office of Comptroller of the Currency.

Washington January 10 1890

by satisfactory evidence presented to the undersigned it has been made to appear that "The Hazleton National Bank," in the Borough Hazleton in the County of Luzerne and State of Pennsylvania has complied with all the provisions of the ~~Revised~~ Statutes of the United States, required to be complied with before an association shall be authorized to commence the business of Banking.

Now therefore [illegible] Comptroller of the Currency, do hereby certify that "The Hazleton National Bank" in the Borough of Hazleton in the County of Luzerne and State of Pennsylvania is authorized to commence the business of Banking as provided in Section Fifty one hundred and sixty nine of the Revised Statutes of the United States.

In testimony whereof witness my hand and Seal of office this 10th day of January 1890.

[illegible]
Deputy and Acting Comptroller of the Currency.

No. 4204

Original charter-1890.

A.S.Van Wickle, a Brown University graduate, came to Hazleton to work for his father at the Ebervale and South Mountain Coal Company which was owned by Ario Pardee. Van Wickle, a descendent of the Randolph family of Virginia, married Bessie Pardee in 1882.

Original main office.

Wilkes University

With a faculty-student ratio of 14:1, Wilkes University offers students individual instruction and hands-on experience. Dr. Sid Halsor, an assistant professor of GeoEnvironmental Sciences and Engineering, assists Julie DePue with a new computer program.

Bucknell University Junior College was established in 1933 to make education available to the families of the Northeastern Pennsylvania coal industry. Sensing a need for greater employment opportunities and advanced education for their children, the business and civic leaders of Wilkes-Barre petitioned Bucknell University in Lewisburg to help them establish a center of higher education for the region.

Lead from the early days of B.U.J.C. by Dr. Eugene S. Farley, the school began to acquire mansions from the Conyngham, Stark, Weckesser, and Kirby families. A library, theater, classrooms, and the president's residence were located in these homes and carriage houses. Former bedrooms served as practice rooms for music students. Fitness sessions and theatrical performances were held on the lawns behind the homes.

The Burns Alumni Tower and Carillon serves as a focal point of Wilkes University's campus, located along the banks of the Susquehanna River.

In 1947, the trustees of Bucknell University relinquished control of the Junior College when it became Wilkes College, a four-year, independent school. "This is not a casual institution, put here lightly. It was built out of faith in you. Faith that you will use these facilities in service to your fellow man," said former Bucknell University president and trustee of Wilkes College Arnaud C. Marts during Charter Day ceremonies on June 26, 1947.

The end of World War II and the advent of the G.I. Bill created a post-war student boom at the College. Many buildings were added to accommodate the new students and growing curriculum. The science and engineering departments were established during this era.

The 1960s were also an era of prosperity for Wilkes. Graduate programs in business, education and the sciences were developed to help attract new companies to the region. The Dorothy Dickson Darte Center for the Performing Arts, the Eugene S. Farley Library, and a new athletic field and facilities were built during the decade to meet the needs of the growing student body.

The devastation created by the Hurricane Agnes flood in 1972 was a catalyst for renewal and reform for Wilkes College. A $13 million check from the government was delivered personally by President Richard Nixon, and hours of work by faculty, students, and the community, reduced the time the university was closed. Though several buildings were lost to the flood, an expansion of the Stark Learning Center was completed and classes resumed in the fall just a few weeks later.

In the 1980s, the college was divided into three distinct units, the School of Science and Engineering, the School of Liberal Arts and Human Sciences, and the School of Business, Society and Public Policy. In 1990, under the leadership of Dr. Christopher N. Breiseth, the school's fourth president, Wilkes achieved University status.

Offering 38 bachelor's and 7 master's study programs, Wilkes continues to develop its curriculum in response to the needs of the community. Following an earlier initiative to educate physicians for work in rural areas of Pennsylvania, Wilkes, in conjunction with the Hahnemann University School of Medicine, and the Guthrie Healthcare System, offers an integrated medical program from freshman year through residency. In 1994 Wilkes launched a six-year Doctor of Pharmacy degree program.

In partnership with King's College and the University of Missouri at Rolla, Wilkes University has spearheaded the Earth Conservancy Project, a non-profit organization formed to restore environmentally damaged land and create new industries.

Leadership roles in teacher education, science and international programs, and the recently formed Allan P. Kirby Center for Free Enterprise and Entrepreneurship all contribute to Wilkes University's identity as "the private university with a public mission." The constant focus on community reflects the deep and continuing commitment of Wilkes University to the people of the region.

The William L. Evans Residence Hall and the Conyngham Student Center are shown from the River Commons. The buildings of the Wilkes campus are primarily turn of the century mansions and homes donated to the University and used as offices, classrooms, and residence halls.

WBRE-TV

WBRE-TV roots edge back to the heyday of radio when "Little" Bill Phillips, Jerry Butler and Phil Cusick broadcast the games of the Wilkes-Barre Barons "live" from Artillery Park in Kingston.

At noon on January 1, 1953 WBRE-TV became the first television station serving Luzerne County and the surrounding Pennsylvania northeast. The 15-minute "live" broadcast, "Welcome to Television," featured Mr. Baltimore, Wilkes-Barre Mayor Luther Kniffen and William O. Sword, chairman of the Committee of 100. Then, ten thousand households stayed tuned as the new TV station broadcast the Tournament of Roses parade, the Cotton and Orange bowls.

During the growth years of television, gaps in the daily coverage of the national networks had to be covered by local shows. One of the most popular was WBRE-TV "Kitchen Magic."

Franklin D. Coslett, who began working for WBRE as a high school student at the age of 16, became the station anchorman and continued until retirement in 1981.

During his life he saw TV transformed from a studio-anchored-medium, with its heavy awkward tube cameras, to today's hand-held camcorders and microwave transmissions bringing events into homes as they were taking place.

The 1972 Agnes Flood devastated WBRE-TV studios and until rebuilding could take place the station operated from its transmitter on Wyoming Mountain.

Charles Sakoski, Sr., who was engineering director when Agnes struck, supervised the staff as they moved much of the station's equipment to Wyoming Mountain. When the call to evacuate Wilkes-Barre came, WBRE-TV and WBRE-FM became the link to the people broadcasting "live" coverage and public service announcements.

In 1976 Louis Baltimore died and his son David Baltimore, assumed direction of the family-owned station.

WBRE-AM was sold in 1978 and two years later WBRE-FM also was sold. The TV station continued under the direction of David Baltimore until August of 1984 when it was sold to Northeastern Television Investors for $21 million.

Disaster struck the new owners on January 8, 1989 when WBRE-TV operating tower fell due to harsh weather. The station continued to operate but it wasn't until October that full power was resumed.

Since 1994 WBRE-TV's 3.02 million watts transmitter carries signals that can be seen by more than two million viewers in 22 counties in the Northeast.

Seated is the late Franklin D. Coslett. Standing from left to right are Fritz Chamberlain and Bob Schumacher.

Present and past anchormen and newscasters–From left to right, Kevin Lynn, Pat Flynn, Franklin D. Coslett and Keith Martin, present anchorman. Mr. Coslett was the first anchorman in Northeastern Pennsylvania and witnessed the growth of area TV from its early stages until his death on February 13, 1992.

Martz

Frank Martz Henry, grandson of the founder was responsible for the recent growth of the Martz Companies.

Martz Lines was started as the White Transit Company in 1908 by Frank Martz, Sr. He began by operating small trucks used to take passengers from Plymouth, Pennsylvania to the nearby mining towns. He bought and supervised the construction of a White 1912 Bus that is still in use today as a museum piece. As the oldest operating antique bus in the country it has won many awards. The White Transit Company expanded routes in 1912 to include local city routing throughout the region until it was sold to the Luzerne County Transportation Authority in 1974.

In 1922 Mr. Martz founded the Frank Martz Coach Company for interstate service. By 1927, the company was operating between Wilkes-Barre and New York City - Philadelphia - Albany - Syracuse - Buffalo - Cleveland - Detroit and Chicago. By 1926, Martz also operated airline service between New York and Buffalo. This service was discontinued in 1933 as economic times worsened. Concentrating on a need for a national transportation system, Frank Martz, Sr. was one of the founders of the National Trailways Bus System. This system through alliances with other independent carriers set schedules and fares for connecting service coast to coast.

Upon the death of Frank Martz, Sr. in 1936, his son, Frank Martz, Jr., assumed control and through his leadership the company was able to operate through the depression era. In 1964 Frank Martz, Jr. died in a helicopter accident. Frank Martz Henry, the grandson of the founder, took control of the company. He continued the systematic growth plan of the business that led the company into the 1990s. Scott Henry represents the fourth generation of the family to work for the company. As a family tradition and regional success story, Martz will continue to provide customer-oriented service well into the future.

Acquisition and start-ups have greatly expanded the company, moving it into bus sales and travel agencies, as well as the operation of coach companies and repair operations in seven states and the Nation's capital. Martz employs a total of 600 people, operating in Pennsylvania with the Price and Martz Lines; Washington, D.C. with the Gold and Gray Line Sightseeing Tours; the National Coach Bus Company and National Coach Works in Virginia; and the Gulf Coast Gray Line and First Class Coach Company in Florida.

Frank Martz, Sr. designed the first White Bus.

In addition to bus operations of regular line service, tours, and charters, Martz opened its own travel agency in Wilkes-Barre in 1984. A Scranton location was added in 1994. These agency locations provide air and cruise service as well as individual and group tour services. The growth and success of the Frank Martz Coach Company has come through the dedication of its many employees and the support of the Wyoming Valley.

Glen Summit Springs Water

In a glen, on a summit about 1800 feet high, deep in the forested Nescopeck Mountain bubbles the crystal-clear water of the Glen Summit Springs. This source has provided delicious, pure spring water that many have been enjoying since 1884.

The Glen Summit area had been, in its heyday, a gathering place for the elite from as far as New York and Philadelphia. Members of the "Wyoming Valley Anthracite Aristocracy" built enormous Victorian cottages at Glen Summit Springs and enjoyed a very active summer social season which included stage coach rides to neighboring areas, tennis, and elaborate parties. People were invited to travel by Lehigh Valley trains to the sprawling grand hotel at Glen Summit, and to enjoy the mountain air and "Purest Spring Water."

The founder of the Glen Summit Springs Water Company, J.E. Patterson, was a successful Wilkes-Barre businessman who was also a very active member of the Glen Summit colony and owner of one of the cottages. Self-described as an undisputed water connoisseur, he often spoke and wrote about the joys of Glen Summit Springs Water. He admitted that he might be a 'crank' when it came to the topic of pure water as a beverage, but preferred to think of himself as a 'philanthropist', doing his best to bring "Nature's greatest gift to man." He established the Glen Summit Springs Water Company in 1884. By the early 1890s, Glen Summit Springs Water was an area favorite. Luzerne County saw the expansion of the company to all points. Patterson even shipped by rail to many metropolitan markets.

In the early 1930's, William Richard Quin, a native of Wilkes-Barre, graduate of Mercersburg Academy, Lafayette College, and chief engineer of the Lake Wallenpaupack Dam project, purchased the Glen Summit Springs Water Company. Under the Quin family's ownership, the company grew and expanded. Mr. Quin added bottled beverages. Made with the spring water, they became popular throughout the region. The spring water occasionally enjoyed recognition on a national level and was sometimes shipped as far as England. Many local people will recall the "seal of purity" logo on the sides of the Glen Summit Springs Water orange delivery trucks.

Today, the water is bottled much the same as at the turn of the century. The water emanates from natural underground springs which stay a constant 45°F. The bottling house, located on its original site, adheres to strict standards to ensure the traditional purity and high quality that J.D. Patterson established so many years ago.

After the death of William Quin in 1972, his widow, Ruth Wicks Quin, and their daughter, Nancy Quin Davis, took on the operation of the firm. Mrs. Davis now maintains the ownership of Glen Summit Springs Water Company with very little change to this family operation. Glen Summit Springs water continues to be a trusted tradition enjoyed by young and old alike.

J.E. Patterson, founder of the company.

The second bottling house still used today.

Glen Summit Springs Hotel circa late 1800's.

Lawrence, Mazzoni and Company

Robert G. Lawrence, CPA, CFP and Joseph R. Mazzoni, CPA.

After many years of experience in large metropolitan areas with two of the accounting industry's major international firms, both Bob Lawrence and Joe Mazzoni saw their individual careers drawn together by many changes. The accounting and financial industries were subject to growth and expansion along with technological advancement during the 1980s. Commercial and industrial prosperity and a positive business environment in the Northeastern Pennsylvania region made opportunities available to both future partners. They returned to the Wyoming Valley ready to employ this experience in their own accounting practices. Both established themselves in sole practitioner positions that would quickly require consolidation to stay ahead of the rapidly developing business climate in the region. Seeing the need for an expanded practice to better serve their individual clients, Lawrence, Mazzoni and Company was formed in 1989.

Bob Lawrence is the Firm's managing partner. He establishes policy for the Firm and maintains the Firm's relationship with clients. Bob is also a certified financial planner and utilizes this expertise in dealing with clients' tax and financial concerns.

As the Firm's accounting and auditing partner, Joe Mazzoni concentrates on the various facets and aspects of this part of the Firm's practice. Joe is also responsible for the Firm's commitment to quality service. He sees to it that the Firm meets the professional standards necessary to maintain its excellent standing in the accounting community.

The diversity of the Firm comes in the form of assistance in planning and consulting with start-up businesses, as well as tax planning and preparation, financial planning and auditing services. Its commitment to professional standards and expertise has enabled Lawrence, Mazzoni and Company to represent a wide variety of businesses and individuals in the region.

MMI Preparatory School

"Old Main" at 154 Centre Street, Freeland, PA.

MMI Preparatory School, formerly the Mining and Mechanical Institute, was founded in 1879 by Eckley B. Coxe as a night school to teach arithmetic, fundamental science and English to boys and young men who worked in the anthracite mines of Eastern Pennsylvania's "middle coal fields."

In 1902, with the completion of the main building, at its present location, the school began to specialize in college preparatory work.

MMI Preparatory School became coeducational in September 1970. In 1977, the middle school for seventh and eighth-grade students was established.

In 1980, the beginning of our second centennial year, MMI's Century II Building opened its doors. This major addition doubled the academic physical plant and offered generous space for the Lambert E. Broad Library, five classrooms and a cafetorium complete with stage and kitchen.

MMI offers the traditional college preparatory curriculum. All Mid-School students take two years of Latin, in addition to English, social studies, math and science. High school courses are developmental, proceeding from a review of general topics to highly specialized courses in the junior and senior year. Major courses are supplemented with specific minor courses to enrich the core curriculum.

MMI Prep is open to any person regardless of race, color, sex, religious preference or national origin. An admissions committee reviews each applicant's qualifications, based on the following:

- Student application form;
- Information sheet;
- Recommendations;
- Results of personal interview;
- Results of entrance exam showing general ability, vocabulary, reading comprehension and mathematics achievement.

Pennsylvania Gas and Water Company

The origins of Pennsylvania Gas and Water Company date back to the 1850's when anthracite coal was king in the Wyoming Valley. Mass quantities of water were needed by coal companies to "wash" the coal in preparation for market, therefore many small water companies operated in the area. For several years, these small water companies were adequate for the local demand, but by 1896, the owners of 29 water companies realized that their supply sources and distribution systems were inadaquate to meet the needs of a growing residential population and for future industrial expansion. Thus, the Spring Brook Water Supply Company was formed to become the parent company through the acquisition of these 29 firms. At the same time, a consolidation of gas and water firms was taking place in the Lackawanna County area. The Scranton Gas and Water Company emerged as the surviving company of the merger of an additional 29 gas and water firms. Gas at that time was manufactured from the burning of coal. Eventually, in 1955 and 1956, the change from manufactured gas to natural gas was accomplished through the construction of a 42 mile transmission line which connected the company's gas system to an interstate natural gas pipeline. By 1956, all of the company's gas customers were being supplied with natural gas.

On October 1, 1960, the combination of a total of 76 forerunner firms culminated in the formation of Pennsylvania Gas and Water Company. In 1974, the company reorganized and formed a holding company, Pennsylvania Enterprises, Inc. (PEI), which owns all of the stock of PG&W and its other minor subsidiaries. PG&W is an investor-owned public utility with assets at December 31, 1993 of approximately $726 million. Currently, employees number 975 people, with a payroll of more than $28.5 million per year.

Through its water division, PG&W serves 132,000 customers in 62 municipalities, including the cities of Wilkes-Barre and Scranton. The water industry has experienced significant change in recent years due to the enactment of the Safe Drinking Water Act and other stringent regulations. To address these regulations, over the past decade PG&W undertook an aggressive program to provide high quality filtered water by building 8 state-of-the-art water treatment plants at a cost expected to exceed $172 million. The company now serves water, which meets or exceeds all state and Federal standards, to 100% of its water customers.

PG&W's natural gas division has expanded substantially since its inception in the late 1950's, providing residential, commercial and industrial customers with efficient, affordable natural gas. Presently, PG&W supplies natural gas to 137,000 customers in 119 municipalities, including the cities of Wilkes-Barre, Scranton and Williamsport. Natural gas has many advantages over other energy sources. Its lower emissions and higher efficiency make natural gas the fuel of choice for many users. With increased technological advances in the natural gas market and heightened awareness of the environment, PG&W's gas operations have potential for great future expansion.

PG&W also plays a major role in the Wyoming Valley by providing vital utilities to attract new industry to the area, and by making non-watershed land available for economic development.

Community involvement is also a very important part of the operations of PG&W. The company's Board of Directors, chaired by Kenneth L. Pollock, is comprised of prominent businessmen and community leaders from throughout PG&W's service territory. Company President, Dean T. Casaday, has placed a priority on programs which focus on assisting people with their needs. The company is deeply involved in United Way campaigns throughout its service area, raising over $100,000 annually through employee contributions. PG&W's Project Outreach Program raises funds from local citizens, businesses and employees to assist needy families in paying their fuel bills. Contributions are matched dollar for dollar by the company. PG&W also participates in Leadership Wilkes-Barre, a program which seeks and trains individuals to be community leaders.

For well over 100 years, the company has played a significant role in the development of the Wyoming Valley. PG&W, with its state-of-the-art water operations, ever expanding gas services and team of dedicated employees, is truly poised to meet the needs of a growing Northeastern Pennsylvania as we enter the next century.

The Genetti Hospitality Group

Damiano Genetti

The Genetti family has established a name for themselves in the Northeastern Pennsylvania hospitality field with a strong focus and commitment to service and community. The family's local history began in 1904, when Damiano Genetti left his home in the Tyrolean Alps (present day Italy), to begin a new life for himself and generations to follow.

Trained as a butcher, he began selling his freshly cured beef door-to-door daily from his horse-drawn wagon. Eventually, his hard work ethic led to an eighteen-store supermarket chain owned and operated by his sons (until it was sold in 1967 to Victory Markets). In addition to sharing his knowledge of food preparation, he shared with his sons the importance of community involvement, honesty, and dedication, before he returned to his homeland shortly after World War I.

In 1950, his son, Gus Sr., and his wife, Della, ventured into the hospitality field by opening the Gus Genetti Hotel and Restaurant in Hazleton. Once the couple developed a business renowned for fine food and service, they expanded the family enterprise further by purchasing the Redington Hotel in Wilkes-Barre in 1963.

Passing his talent and expertise on to the next generation, Gus Sr. sold his interest in the Wilkes-Barre property to Gus Jr. in 1971 and his interest in the Hazleton property to his son, Bill, in 1973. Gus Sr. passed away in 1976 and Della earlier that same year.

Expanding further, Gus Jr. acquired the Lycoming Hotel in Williamsport in 1975 and developed Genetti Manor in Dickson City. His brother, Bill, improved and expanded the original property in Hazleton.

As of this writing, the Genetti Hospitality Group, owned by Bill and Gus Genetti, Jr., is comprised of the Best Western Genetti Motor Lodge - Hazleton, Best Western Genetti Hotel and Convention Center - Wilkes-Barre, Genetti Hotel and Convention Center - Williamsport, and Genetti Manor, a catering facility in Dickson City. In each of these markets, the Genetti brothers have maintained a strong presence in the hospitality field, including the largest banquet facilities of the area, the largest being Wilkes-Barre, seating 1,800 people in one ballroom.

Although many things have changed since the years of the horse-drawn meat wagon, the dedication to food quality and the importance of service instituted by Damiano is still evident and maintained by the Genetti family today. The fourth generation of Genettis is already hard at work in the food and hospitality industry.

Being in business in Luzerne County through this century has not been without its trials and tribulations. Fires, hurricanes, wars, and (pictured above) a flood in downtown Wilkes-Barre caused by Tropical Storm Agnes in late June of 1972. Hotel guests are being evacuated by the Pennsylvania National Guard after the Susquehanna River breached the dikes and flooded downtown Wilkes-Barre. The depth of water surrounding the hotel was 8 feet.

A meat wagon used by Damiano and his four sons to deliver to the residents of Hazleton. (Currently on display at the Pennsylvania Anthracite Heritage Museum in Scranton, PA).

One of several bakery trucks used to deliver Genetti's quality bakery products, circa 1930.

Gus Genetti, Sr.

Bill Genetti

Gus Genetti, Jr.

Gus Genetti, Sr. inspecting mink pelts. Mink breeding played a large part in the Genetti family enterprises with Gus Genetti, Sr. receiving international recognition for developing new colors through genetic development and raising quality mink at the Genetti Mink Ranch in the Sugarloaf Valley.

The grand opening of the Genetti Supermarket, Laurel Street, Hazleton, one of the most modern supermarkets in the United States at that time. It featured automatic door openers operated by an electric eye. Quite a novelty in 1939. From left: Al, Gus, Stanley, and Leon Genetti.

Franklin First Savings Bank

Franklin First
Main Office
44 W. Market St.
Wilkes-Barre, PA

Franklin First Savings Bank's operations began on June 25, 1934 with one employee doing business from a rented window in the Hanover National Bank and assets of $5,300.

A long line of merges has left Franklin as the predominant savings bank in Luzerne County with 22 branch offices serving a six-county area that extends from Stroudsburg in the Poconos, to Tunkhannock in the Endless Mountains, and up and down the Susquehanna from Old Forge to Berwick.

While keeping its identity, the latest merger with ONBANCorp will open to the customers of Franklin the added services of a trust office, expanded commercial lending and the management of pension funds and estates.

Franklin's tremendous growth and success can be attributed to its philosophy of "sticking to the basics" that originated with its first president, Henry Weigand, and was carried on by Alexander J. Boetiger, Elmer J. Klimchak and Thomas H. van Arsdale.

Over forty years ago, Franklin's strong growth caused the 14 member board of directors to select a location on South Main Street, Wilkes-Barre for the institution's first office. After several moves the board in 1951 selected the present site at 44 West Market Street in Wilkes-Barre. From this location Franklin became the leading provider of residential mortgages in Northeastern Pennsylvania.

The first branch office was opened at the Gateway Shopping Center in February 1959. By 1973 four branches were added with the merger of the Berwick Savings and Loan Association. By 1978 mergers added another 12 offices and in 1982 the First Federal Savings and Loan Association was merged into Franklin.

By the early 1990's, Franklin established three loan offices in the Poconos at Hawley, Pocono Summit and Clarks Summit.

Another significant change that furthered Franklin's growth was the deregulation of the banking industry in the early 1980's which produced fierce competition and allowed savings and loans to offer products and services similar to that offered by commercial banks. The deregulation brought about the crisis of the 1980's that ended with the famous bail out from the federal government and the Federal Deposit Insurance Corporation.

Franklin, however prospered and was ranked in the top 20 percent of the nation's savings and loans in 1990 and continues its tradition of high performance to this day.

Item processing department.

Teller training in progress.

Teller/Customer.

"Franklin First has served as a community bank in Northeastern Pennsylvania for over half a century. We are proud of our staff's dedication to providing outstanding customer service and to their extensive involvement in community activities which help to enhance the quality of life of our fellow citizens."

Quote from Thomas H. Van Arsdale
President & CEO
Franklin First Savings Bank

RJR Nabisco

When cracker and cookie giant RJR Nabisco purchased Planters Peanuts and Chocolate Company in 1961, many Luzerne County residents predicted another home-grown industry was about to be shut down and moved out of Wilkes-Barre.

As it turned out, however, Nabisco had other plans for its new acquisition. The company built a modern 160,000 square foot "back office" in Hanover that now employs 450 people.

Coupling the region's legendary work ethic with a fast-paced, nationwide business environment has proven to be good for the company and the community.

Not surprisingly, Nabisco believes in being a good corporate citizen. But unlike many companies whose involvement with the community is limited to top executives and cash contributions, Nabisco executives urge all their employees to donate some of their time to activities in their churches, community projects, colleges, libraries and civic organizations.

Vincent Sortino, vice president of Nabisco Foods Group service center, summed up this community spirit when he said, "We just don't want to be in the community, we want to be a part of the community." Sortino's remarks echo a company philosophy that can be traced all the way back to the founders of Nabisco and Planters Peanuts.

Planters, founded by Amedeo Obici and Mario Peruzzi in Wilkes-Barre in 1906, grew within six years to a multi-million dollar industry. Much of the credit for the success of the firm belongs to Mr. Obici, a master of modern day marketing, who flooded the market with toys and other trinkets advertising the peanut business.

Present site of RJR Nabisco, 50 New Commerce Blvd., Hanover Industrial Estates, Wilkes-Barre.

The beginnings of Nabisco can be traced to 1792 when John Pearson established the first commercial community bakery in the village of Newburyport, Massachusetts. The bakery was family owned for more than 100 years before becoming the National Biscuit Company. Subsequent mergers and acquisitions increased the product lines and a merger with Standard Brands in 1981 created one of the biggest corporations in the nation.

Today, looking toward the technologic and economic landscape of the twenty-first century, Nabisco places great emphasis on educating its employees and their families. Benefit programs are heavily weighted toward education agendas, and on-site, lifestyle programs at the Wilkes-Barre facility emphasize the company's concern for continued education.

The company encourages and supports innovative education programs in school districts nationwide. It helps employees educate their children with a Scholastic Saving Plan that matches employees' savings. It fosters involvement in local communities by matching an employee's personal contribution to certain educational institutions. It also encourages employees to enhance their business-related skills and knowledge through a tuition reimbursement benefit.

For families, the facility promotes its Parent/Education Task Force, whose motto is "You Are The Key To Your Children's Success And An Integral Part Of The Education Process." A full slate of programs includes on-site book fairs, seminars, the Nabisco-wide Summer Reading Adventure as well as tours of the facility for area school groups.

Additionally, the Nabisco facility in Wilkes-Barre plays an active community leadership role through internships for local colleges, job fairs, mentor programs with the Northeastern Network, participation in Junior Achievement, Scouting, Head Start, Project Learn and sponsorship of the Philharmonic Children's Concert.

And there's more!

Each year Nabisco employees lend their time and expertise to the United Way. Probably its most remarkable community oriented project, the facility is justifiably proud of its 100 percent participation by its employees in United Way.

Nabisco — a big part of our community!

Greater Wilkes-Barre Family YMCA

The Wilkes-Barre Young Mens Christian Association was originally formed on May 8, 1863, to foster recreational and religious programs in the community, with the YMCA using various sites in downtown Wilkes-Barre. Agib Ricketts, a lawyer, was the first President of the YMCA Board. However, the nation was engaged in the Civil War, and the local YMCA effort was abandoned after 1864.

In 1871 under President George S. Bennett the YMCA was reorganized and again utilized various sites until 1892 when the YMCA completed construction of a building at 23 North Main Street (the site of the Times Leader). This building had bowling alleys, a gymnasium, and pool. An evening school program, begun in 1878, was the first night school in Wilkes-Barre. At the turn of the century, a mining school was organized. It offered courses in mining techniques and safety, and mining classes were offered for half a century.

In 1903 the YMCA building was renovated following a fire, and in 1911 a boys' building, the former G.J. Stegmaier home next to Coughlin High School, was renovated and enlarged for YMCA use. In 1922 the South Branch was formed at 434 South Main Street in Wilkes-Barre and served the Black community. In time, other branch YMCAs were also opened: Midvale in Plains in 1944, the Memorial branch in Parsons in 1946, and the Back Mountain branch in 1952.

The YMCA began its camping program in 1902 at North Pond, and later at various Susquehanna River sites in Wyoming County, and in 1922 at Lake Moseywood in the Poconos. In 1927-1929 F.M. Kirby and Gilbert McClintock donated a 100 acre site for a boys' summer camp along the Lehigh River near Blakeslee. In 1953 the YMCA left Blakeslee and relocated to an 1,100 acre site near White Haven, named Camp Kresge, after S.S. Kresge who donated the costs of constructing the camp buildings. A summer day camp program is maintained at Frances Slocum State Park in the Back Mountain.

On October 1, 1934, the current YMCA building, was opened at a cost of $625,000. Constructed on the site of the former George S. Bennett mansion, it was designed by architect Thomas A. Foster and built in a remarkable fifteen months, during the depression, by the A.J. Sordini contracting company. The 75 foot swimming pool was dedicated to former Board President Charles F. Clift (1925-1927). Four floors contained 96 bedrooms leased to single men.

The Wilkes-Barre Young Womens Christian Association was formed in 1893 and formally chartered in 1897. In 1910 the YWCA dedicated a new building on North Franklin Street in Wilkes-Barre, adjacent to the now Angeline Kirby Health Center. The YWCA's building campaign was launched with a $10,000.00 gift from J.W. Hollenback, at one time Board President of the YMCA. The upper floors of the YWCA had 40 rooms for both permanent and transient guests. In July 1923 a 60 foot swimming pool was dedicated. From 1931 to 1948 the YWCA operated the Blue Triangle Camp at Harveys Lake.

In October 1961 the Wilkes-Barre YWCA relocated to an enlarged YMCA to jointly serve the community. Later, the YWCA formally dissolved its corporate body, after years of distinguished service to community. From this evolution the Greater Wilkes-Barre Family YMCA emerged.

A member agency of the United Way of Wyoming Valley, the YMCA has a rich history of community service far beyond the recreational facilities it offers. Largely unheralded are its special programs for the disadvantaged, handicapped and area youth, often managed and staffed by the Y's volunteer committees. The YMCA annually honors a Lay Person Of the Year, a prized honor dating from 1935. Among the recipients was Clarence E. Beerweiler ("Mr. YMCA"), manager of the Kresge store on Public Square, and a Y volunteer for 50 years. The Rodgers Basketball Tournament has run continuously since 1932, honoring the Y's first athletic director W.A. Rodgers (1906-1931).

During its long history only fourteen executive directors (formerly general secretaries) have served the Y. F.M. Devendorf served an incredible term from 1912 to 1940. Well-known in later years was Eric H. Planitzer (1957-1976), and the beloved Bernard J Hargadon (1978-1994) whose tenure marks the YMCA in modern times.

The YM-YWCA, corner W. Northampton and S. Franklin Sts., Wilkes-Barre, in 1964.

The YMCA celebrated the 90th birthday of "Mr. YMCA," Clarence E. Beerweiler, in September 1991. Left to right, Andrew Shaw, Jr., Board President; Beerweiler; Louise Dickinson, Program Director; Bernard J. Hargadon, Executive Director.

Wyoming Valley Health Care System

Shown at the affiliation signing between Wilkes-Barre General Hospital and Nesbitt Memorial Hospital in September 1992 are, from left, John D. McCarthy, former chairman of the Wilkes-Barre General Hospital Board of Directors and current chairman of the Wyoming Valley Health Care System Board of Directors; Ron Stern, former president and chief executive officer of Nesbitt Memorial Hospital and current president and chief executive officer of Wyoming Valley Health Care System; and Dr. Ralph B Rozelle, former chairman of the Nesbitt Memorial Hospital Board of Directors and current vice chairman of the Wyoming Valley Health Care System Board of Directors.

Steeped in tradition and predicated on an ever-growing commitment to improve the quality and availability of health care services in northeastern Pennsylvania, Wyoming Valley Health Care System and its related affiliates continue in their Vision to become the leader in providing and managing quality health care services to meet the region's needs in a compassionate, collaborative, and cost-effective manner.

This Vision has provided the framework and direction for this health care System that has experienced tremendous growth and made significant progress since the formal merger of Nesbitt Memorial Hospital and Wilkes-Barre General Hospital in September 1992.

Since its founding in October 1872 as the Wilkes-Barre City Hospital, Wilkes-Barre General Hospital has for over 120 years experienced and adapted to the many changes that have occurred both in the medical world and the community it serves.

Nesbitt Memorial Hospital was known as the Nesbitt West Side Hospital when it opened its doors for patient admission and treatment in October 1912. For over 80 years, it has consistently demonstrated the highest standards of concern for the health care needs of community residents.

With over 3,500 full- and part-time employees and a medical staff comprised of over 450 skilled physicians, compassionate, technologically-advanced medical and surgical services are provided via an integrated health care delivery System that has responded to the region's needs for over 200 years.

While aligning itself with other health care providers in the area, Wyoming Valley Health Care System has embraced the concept of consolidating existing services and creating new, innovative programs to ensure that affordable, quality, and superior medical care will be available in this region — now and into the future.

"The respective boards of directors of Nesbitt Memorial Hospital and Wilkes-Barre General Hospital anticipated the significant changes in the delivery of health care services which are now occurring," explains Ron Stern, president and chief executive officer of Wyoming Valley Health Care System.

"These board members enacted positive change instead of letting uncertainties in health care dictate the degree and sophistication of health care services these proud institutions could offer area residents. The creation of Wyoming Valley Health Care System is a testimony both to their foresight and faith in the physicians, employees, volunteers, and auxilians who have served both hospitals so well."

"Both hospital boards of directors saw the future of health care resting in collaboration and elimination of duplicate services," adds John D. McCarthy, chairman of the Board of Directors of Wyoming Valley Health Care System. "These dedicated volunteers realized the practicality of joining resources, and together, created a health care network that will help ensure the continuance of quality, compassionate medical services for which both hospitals have distinguished themselves in Wyoming Valley."

Today, Wyoming Valley Health Care System is the region's leader in the delivery of sophisticated, technologically-advanced services. Among the medical and surgical specialties available through the System are a respected Cardiac Surgery program, featuring Open Heart and other cardiac surgical procedures, cardiology program, obstetrical and gynecological services, cardiac care services, women's and children's services, a comprehensive cancer care program, assorted general surgical procedures, including same day surgical procedures such as diagnostic laparoscopy, arthroscopy, septoplasty, and bronchoscopy; dialysis services, advanced medical services, short stay procedures, and diagnostic and therapeutic services.

Wyoming Valley Health Care System also addresses the community's needs from the traditional medical perspective to services and programs for patients both prior to the onset of illness or disease and following inpatient treatment. Commitment to enhancement activities which foster healthy living is evidenced through innovative preventive health management services, ambulatory care centers, corporate health services, physical medicine services, cardiac rehabilitation, fitness and nutrition programs, health enhancement services which emphasize preventive health issues for the community and work force, health awareness and staff enhancement programs, and family outreach community services.

During 1994, the Berwick Healthcare Corporation, Visiting Nurse Association/Home Health Services, Inc., and Community Counseling Services of NE PA affiliated themselves with Wyoming Valley Health Care System. These respected community resources will further ensure the continued delivery and provision of cost-effective, quality health care services both in the greater Wyoming Valley and Berwick areas.

Affiliated entities of Wyoming Valley Health Care System include General Medical Services Corporation, Heritage House, Rural Health Corporation of Northeastern Pennsylvania, United Health and Hospital Services, Susquehanna Management Services, Inc. (CHOICES), and Susquehanna Mobile Health Services, Inc.

Over the years, both hospital campuses have adapted to the many changes that have occurred both in the world of medicine and the community each serves. Collectively, the Nesbitt Memorial Hospital and Wilkes-Barre General Hospital campuses, their entities and all affiliates demonstrate the highest standards of concern for the health care of area residents, with compassion and caring ever present as the principal philosophies of the corporate entity, Wyoming Valley Health Care System.

Valley Automobile Club

The Valley Automobile Club, 100 Hazle Street, Wilkes-Barre.

"The purpose for which the corporation is formed is the maintenance of a Club for social enjoyment, the promotion of motoring, and to promote, aid, and support the movement for the improvement of highways."

These aims of the Valley Automobile Club were contained in its petition for incorporation to Judge George S. Ferris in the Court of Common Pleas in Luzerne County on May 8, 1908.

The original club was named the Wilkes-Barre Automobile Club.

The club's name was changed to the Wyoming Valley Motor Club in 1959 and in 1965, merged which resulted in the name change to The Valley Automobile Club.

The club offers a wide variety of service to its members, including emergency road service, bail and arrest bonds, automobile routing, notary, license, and title services.

The Valley Automobile Club and its parent organization, the AAA, together operate the largest travel agency in the world. The club can arrange travel by plane, ship, and rail. It also can take care of details such as customs, immigration regulations, passport assistance, tours, hotel reservations, and traveler's cheques.

Personal accident and travel insurance, including baggage, flight, and trip cancellation and interruption, are available from the club as well.

In its support of the community and motoring safety, the Valley Automobile Club conducts programs in schools, issues safety posters and lesson plans, and organizes safety patrols and equips them with badges and belts. In conjunction with its parent organization, the club maintains and loans a safety film library, and provides traffic, pedestrian, and bicycle safety programs.

Murray Realty and Rentals

The Wilkes-Barre Lace Corporation structure in North Wilkes-Barre.

Murray Realty and Rentals officially formed in 1958, but its underpinnings were carefully being planned by its owner eleven years earlier. Thomas J. Murray, Jr. started his first business fresh out of high school and ready to work. His painting and construction jobs quickly established him in a reliable and reputable business. Murray Construction became the forerunner of the current company, expanding its work throughout the state.

Tom Murray began the real estate company with the purchase of the Cumberland Apartments in Wilkes-Barre. Built in 1906, it was for its time the tallest structure in the city. It housed 58 aprtments and became the cornerstone of the firm. Growth in the business had the company managing close to 400 rental units by the late 1960's.

The Flood of 1972, along with the demise of mining and overall economic downturn in the area led the Murray Realty and Rental Company to a new phase in its development. Existing factories and manufacturing sites in the region whose usefulness had since been replaced or eliminated began to lay empty. Murray began to purchase and renovate several historical structures starting with the Wilkes-Barre Lace Corporation property in 1973. As the residential aspect of Murray Realty diminished, the commercial side began to prosper. Murray added a second property in 1974 when he made the purchase of the Hazard Wire and Rope factory in Wilkes-Barre a part of the renovation concept.

Today the buildings reflect the Murrays' dedication to providing revitaliztion to historic structures as mixed use needs are dictated by the current economic trends. The Okonite Corporation's Hazard Wire and Rope factory now houses mercatile office space with mixed light manufacturing and the Murray Realty and Rental Company's latest enterprise-Murray's Inn. A dream of both Tom Murray, Jr. and his son Thomas Joseph Murray, III, the restaurant stands as a testimony to the determination and hard work ethic the entire Murray family espouses. Their desire to bring a quality eating establishment to the downtown area has allowed the Murray family enterprises to grow, effectively demonstrating the multipurpose advantages of historical renovation.

As the company's president, Thomas J. Murray, III continues to operate the family's holdings with the same drive and determination his father initiated. Together, Tom Murray, Jr. and his son manage the Inn and the growing list of Murray Realty and Rental Properties.

The old Hazard Wire and Rope Complex that now houses Murray's Inn and mercantile office space.

King's College

As King's College nears its fiftieth anniversary it still remains dedicated to its founding principles of academic excellence rooted in a core curriculum of general studies.

It's emphasis on core curriculum has been cited by several national academic associations as a model curriculum incorporating traditional and new concepts in liberal arts education.

Students can choose from 35 major programs in business, humanities, social sciences and natural science. In addition, graduate programs in finance, health care administration, accounting and taxation were introduced during the 1990s.

An independent Catholic college founded in 1946 by the Congregation of Holy Cross from the University of Notre Dame, King's received its state charter on May 6, 1946, and the first class of 300 men attended classes in a recently renovated building on West Northampton Street in Wilkes-Barre.

Father James W. Connerton, C.S.C., the first president, with the assistance of Father William Scandlon, C.S.C., and Father Patrick Duffy, C.S.C., set about building a college.

It was a difficult time for a college or any institution to begin operation. World War II had ended one year earlier and the nation was just beginning to turn around from war to peace-time production. Building materials and even chairs, chalkboards and textbooks were in scarce supply.

Robert Ell, a graduate of St. Nicholas High School, was the first student to pay the $200 tuition fee. Following graduation, Ell became alumni and placement director and 42 years later retired as Director of Alumni Relations at King's.

As the years passed, King's moved to its current location and expanded tremendously from that humble beginning. Now, King's enrolls more than 2,300 full and part-time students and employs more than 100 full-time faculty members.

King's recently completed its most successful capital campaign, raising more than $22 million for the construction of the $7 million William G. McGowan School of Business, the development of 33.5 acres for a new outdoor athletic complex, the completion of the $6.4 million Charles E. and Mary Parente Life Sciences Center and for funds for student scholarship assistance and faculty development.

King's value and academic reputation were recognized by *U.S. News and World Report* and *Barron's Best Buys in College Education*. *U.S. News*, in its 1995 Annual Best Colleges Guide, ranked King's eighth among Regional Liberal Arts Colleges in the northern United States. King's was listed in *Barron's* for the second consecutive edition.

According to *Barron's* "A King's College degree in any of several well-respected professional fields will almost ensure an excellent first job after graduation; a King's College education, through the comprehensive core curriculum, will provide sustenance throughout a graduate's life."

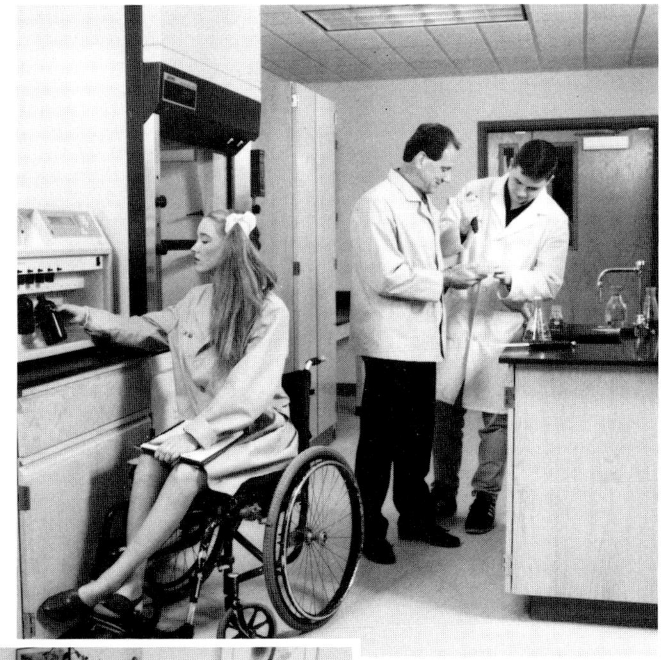

Dr. Robert Paoletti, chairperson of Biology, (center), works on a research project with students in the new Parente Life Sciences Center.

The Reverend William Condon, C.S.C., Vice President for Student Affairs, talks with students in John Lane House.

The Greater Wilkes-Barre Chamber of Commerce

110 Years of Service, 1884-1994.

Over the course of the past 110 years, the Wyoming Valley has changed dramatically. Things that many probably thought would be around forever are nothing more than memories. Gone are the horse drawn carriages and the early steam locomotives. Also gone are many early industries--the coal mines and smokestack industries--that helped build a region that we are proud to call home. But even with all that change, some things have remained the same. First, the spirit of the Valley's early citizens is still strong in its modern residents. Dedicated to their families and their communities, these descendents of those that built the "Valley With a Heart" have joined with newcomers to continue the tradition of welcoming all and creating opportunities for residents to build a bright future.

Along with that, over the course of the past eleven decades, the effort to improve our region put forth by the business community through the Greater Wilkes-Barre Chamber of Commerce has been a constant. From the organization's beginnings in 1884 as the Board of Trade, the Chamber has evolved into a community force that not only encourages the development and growth of commerce and industry but works to improve our entire community.

Today, your Chamber and its volunteers work to make the community better by addressing key issues such as flood protection, 911 emergency services and the Northeastern Pennsylvania Civic and Convention Center. Representing some 1,300 businesses of all types and sizes. the Chamber prides itself on being the recognized "voice of business." Staff and volunteers evaluate legislative proposals as to the effect they would have on maintaining and creating jobs for our citizens. New areas for Chamber involvement have also emerged as times have changed. The Chamber is now actively involved in establishing partnerships between local businesses and schools to provide our future work force with the skills required by employers.

The Chamber, through its affiliated organizations--the Committee for Economic Growth and the Greater Wilkes-Barre Industrial Fund--also works to bring new industries into the Wyoming Valley and to offer existing businesses the opportunity to grow. Through the Industrial Fund, business can locate in one of several modern office and industrial parks throughout the area. The Corporate Center at East Mountain (a high-tech PP&L Ultra-Service[SM] Park), Hanover Industrial Estates, Crestwood and Highland parks offer all the amenities the modern business needs to succeed.

The Committee for Economic Growth serves as the marketing arm of the business community. An aggressive recruitment campaign has resulted in thousands of new jobs for the region--jobs that, for the first time in history, give our young people the opportunity to stay in Northeastern Pennsylvania.

Your Chamber--the Greater Wilkes-Barre Chamber of Commerce--has evolved into a modern, full-service business and community development organization. The founders of the Board of Trade probably never envisioned their young organization becoming so large or so active, or that their initiative of 110 years ago would create an organization with a track record of service that few, if any, can match. The Greater Wilkes-Barre Chamber of Commerce's membership plaque reads "Progress With Tradition." It is that goal that drives the 1,300 members and 400+ volunteers to strive for a better future, while remembering and honoring this region's proud past.

Board of Luzerne County Commissioners

We'd like to take this opportunity to thank the Wyoming Historical and Geological Society for preserving our most precious heritage which this County traditionally honors as it builds for the future.

Signed,
Your Board of Luzerne County Commissioners,
Jim Phillips
Rose S. Tucker, Chair
Frank P. Crossin

BIBLIOGRAPHY

Aurand, Harold W. *From the Molly Maguires to the United Mine Workers: The Social Ecology of an Industrial Union.* Philadelphia: Temple University Press, 1971.

Aurand, Harold W. *Population Change and Social Continuity: Ten Years in a Coal Town.* Selinsgrove, PA: Susquehanna University Press and London: Associated University Presses, 1986.

Berthoff, Rowland Tappan. *British Immigrants in Industrial America: 1790-1950.* Cambridge: Harvard University Press, 1953.

Bradsby, Henry C., ed. *History of Luzerne County, Pennsylvania.* Chicago: I.B. Nelson and Co., 1893.

Cornell, Robert J. *The Anthracite Coal Strikes of 1902.* New York: Russell and Russell, 1971; reprint ed. from 1957.

Davies, Edward J. II. *The Anthracite Aristocracy: Leadership and Social Change in the Hard Coal Regions of Northeastern Pennsylvania.* DeKalb, IL: Northern Illinois University Press, 1985.

Ethnic Heritage Studies: Papers of the Institute at King's College.

Gallagher, John P. *A Century of History: The Diocese of Scranton, 1868-1968.* Scranton: Diocese of Scranton, 1968.

Golab, Caroline. "Impact of the Industrial Experience on the Immigrant Family." Richard L. Ehrlich, ed. *Immigrants in Industrial America.* Charlottesville: University Press of Virginia, 1976

Greene, Victor R. *The Slavic Community on Strike: Immigrant Labor in Pennsylvania Anthracite.* Notre Dame: University of Notre Dame Press, 1968.

Hanlon, Edward F. *The Wyoming Valley: An American Portrait.* Woodland Hills, CA: Windsor Publications, 1983.

Hartmann, Edward G. *The Ethnic Religious Congregations of the Wyoming Valley.* Wilkes-Barre: Osterhout Free Library, 1987.

Hartmann, Edward G. *The Ethnic History of the Wyoming Valley.* Published by the author, 1987.

Harvey, Oscar Jewell (completed by Ernest Gray Smith). *A History of Wilkes-Barre, Luzerne County, Pennsylvania: From Its First Beginnings to the Present Time, Including Chapters of Newly-Discovered Early Wyoming Valley History, Together With Many Biographical Sketches and Much Genealogical Material.* 6 volumes. Wilkes-Barre: Raeder Press, 1909-1930.

Janosov, Robert. "The Auchincloss Mine Disaster of 1904: A Case Study of the Nature of Mine Accidents and Attitudes Towards Them," *The History of Northeastern Pennsylvania: The Last 100 Years. Proceedings of the First Annual Conference at Luzerne County Community College,* 1989.

Kingston, Pennsylvania. A Report of a Community Survey Conducted by Students of Wilkes College. Wilkes-Barre, PA: Kingston Rotary Club, 1955.

Krawczeniuk, Joseph V. *Ukrainians in Luzerne County.* Wilkes-Barre: King's College, 1982.

Lottick, Sally Teller. *Bridging Change: A Wyoming Valley Sketchbook.* Wilkes-Barre, PA: Wyoming Historical and Geological Society, 1992.

Luzerne County Planning Commission documents.

Miller, Donald L. and Richard E. Sharpless. *The Kingdom of Coal: Work, Enterprise and Ethnic Communities in the Mine Fields.* Philadelphia: University of Pennsylvania Press, 1985.

Moss, Emerson I. *African-Americans in the Wyoming Valley, 1778-1990.* Wilkes-Barre: Wyoming Historical and Geological Society and the Wilkes University Press, 1992.

Novak, Michael. *The Guns of Lattimer: The True Story of a Massacre and Trial August 1897-March 1899.* New York: Basic Books, Inc., Publishers, 1979.

Mussari, Anthony J. *Appointment with Disaster.* Wilkes-Barre, PA: Northeast Publishers, 1974.

Petrillo, F. Charles. *Anthracite and Slackwater: The North Branch Canal, 1828-1901.* Easton, PA: Center for Canal History and Technology, 1986.

Petrillo, F. Charles. *Harvey's Lake.* Wilkes-Barre, PA: F.C. Petrillo, 1983.

Ramsauer, Gabrielle, and Economic Development Council of Northeastern Pennsylvania. *Transportation in Northeastern Pennsylvania: 1776 to 1976.* Avoca, PA: Economic Development Council of Northeastern Pennsylvania, 1979.

Roberts, Peter. *Anthracite Coal Communities: A Study of the Demography, the Social and Moral Life of the Anthracite Regions.* Columbus: J.L. Tocuzer Printing Company, 1905; reprint by Westport: Greenwood Press, 1970.

Rose, Dan. *Energy Transition and the Local Community: A Theory of Society Applied to Hazleton, Pennsylvania.* Philadelphia: University of Pennsylvania Press, 1981.

Smith, S.(amuel) R.(obert). *The Wyoming Valley in the Nineteenth Century.* Wilkes-Barre, PA: Wilkes-Barre Leader Printing, 1894.

Spear, Sheldon. *Chapters in Wyoming Valley History: Notable Men, Women, and Events.* Shavertown: Jemags Spear, 1989.

Spear, Sheldon. "High Noon or Twilight," *The History of Northeastern Pennsylvania: The Last 100 Years. Proceedings of the Fourth Annual Conference at Luzerne County Community College,* 1992.

Spear, Sheldon. "Life After Anthracite: Wyoming Valley's Economic Recovery in the 1950s and 1960s," *The History of Northeastern Pennsylvania: The Last 100 Years. Proceedings of the Second Annual Conference at Luzerne County Community College,* 1990.

Spear, Sheldon. "Wyoming Valley During the Great Depression," *The History of Northeastern Pennsylvania: The Last 100 Years. Proceedings of the First Annual Conference at Luzerne County Community College,* 1989.

This Is Luzerne County. Wilkes-Barre: League of Women Voters of the Wilkes-Barre Area and the Hazleton Area, 1976.

This Is Luzerne County, Revised edition. Jane Elmes-Crahall, ed. Wilkes-Barre: League of Women Voters of the Wilkes-Barre Area and the Hazleton Area, 1992.

Turner, George. "The Lattimer Massacre," *The History of Northeastern Pennsylvania: The Last 100 Years. Proceedings of the Second Annual Conference at Luzerne County Community College,* 1990.

United States Bureau of Census. *First through the Fourteenth Census of the United States, 1790-1920.* Washington: Government Printing Office.

United States Bureau of Census. *Fifteenth through the Twenty-first Census of the United States, 1930-1990.*

Valletta, Clement L., "Ritual and Folklife in Pennsylvania's Wyoming Region: Old to New World Wonder," *Pennsylvania Folklife,* Autumn 1983, Vol. 33, No. 1.

Warne, Frank Julian. *The Slav Invasion and the Mine Workers: A Study of Immigration.* Philadelphia: J. B. Lippincott Company, 1904.

Wilkes College. *The Wilkes College History of the Wyoming Valley: Lecture Series, 1986-1987: An Anthology.* Wilkes-Barre, PA: Wilkes College Press, 1989.

Williamson, James R. "The Yankee-Pennamite Wars," *The Proceedings, Middle Atlantic Historical Association of Catholic Colleges and Universities,* Volume VI, 1991.

Wolensky, Robert P. and Flood Recovery Task Force. *Better Than Ever: The Flood Recovery Task Force.* Stevens Point, WI: Foundation Press, 1993.

Zbiek, Paul J. "The Ethnic Heritage of the Wyoming Valley," *The History of Northeastern Pennsylvania: The Last 100 Years. Proceedings of the Fourth Annual Conference at Luzerne County Community College,* 1992.

Zbiek, Paul J. "The Importance of High School Sports in Northeastern Pennsylvania," *The History of Northeastern Pennsylvania: The Last 100 Years. Proceedings of the First Annual Conference at Luzerne County Community College,* 1989.

Zbiek, Paul J. "Products of the Land: Geographic Utilization and Ethnicity in Two Northeastern Pennsylvania Communities, 1800-1880," *The Proceedings, Middle Atlantic Historical Association of Catholic Colleges and Universities,* Volume VI, 1991.

COLOR PICTURE CREDITS: 8, *Reynolds' Woods, Bear Creek,* by Celia Burnham Seymour,courtesy Edward Welles, Jr. Collection, D. Leonard Corgan Library, King's College. 9, *The Village,* by Irving O. Thomas, Welles Collection; *Dial Rock,* by Charles B. Zimmerman, Welles Collection. 64, *Susquehanna River with Market Street Bridge,* by Vince Civiletti, courtesy Luzerne National Bank; photo, Robb Malloy. 65, photos, Robb Malloy; *Luzerne's One Room Schoolhouse,* by Vince Civiletti, Luzerne National Bank. 66, 67, 70, photos, I376. 68, courtesy Luzerne National Bank. 69, photos top and bottom, I376; center, Robb Malloy. 71, courtesy Bohlin, Cywinski, Jackson Architects; photos, Robb Malloy. 72, by Sue Hand, courtesy Luzerne National Bank; photos, I376. 73, photo, George Welch, Jr.; photo, I376; courtesy Luzerne National Bank.

BLACK AND WHITE PICTURE CREDITS: 19, 35, 53, 54, 56, 61, 62, 74, 77, 78, 79, 82, 83, 85, 90, Greater Hazleton Historical Society. 24, Francis D. Garrahan. 25, The Welles Collection, King's College. 38, 43, 47, 50, 79, 83, Ruth Howe. 44, Philip Kelly. 59, 100, 101, 102, 107, I376 Photo. 76, 86, 93, 95-98, 105, Times Leader. 91, HAER Div., National Park Service. 92, Judge Bernard C. Brominski. 92, Luzerne County Medical Society. 99, 100, Fred Ziemer. 104, Slovak Heritage Society of Northeastern Pennsylvania. 105, St. Gabriel's Roman Catholic Church. 106, The Peace Center. 106, The Earth Conservancy. Unless otherwise noted, images are from the Wyoming Historical and Geological Society Collection.

INDEX

A

African Americans 107
Airport 21, 24, 37, 87
Americanization 79
Anthracite industry 14, 34-39, 48, 75, 77, 79, 86, 88, 91, 102
Archeology 21, 24
Ashley 55
Auchincloss disaster 40
Avoca 37

B

Back Mountain 14, 82, 104
Balliet, John 30
Baseball 83
Battle of Wyoming 26-29
Bear Creek 13, 82, 105
Berwick 30
Bethlehem 23
Black lung disease 41, 98
Blue Coal Company 108
Butler Valley 30

C

CAN-DO 18, 92
Canals 35, 36
Carbondale 35
Cefalo, Jimmy 54
Chamber of Commerce 92
Climate 14
Coal 11-19, 33-35, 37-44, 47, 48, 51, 52, 55-57, 59-63, 75, 77, 81, 82, 86-88, 91-94, 98, 99, 101, 102, 106-108
College Misericordia 80, 89, 104
Company towns 18
Connecticut 22-25, 28-30, 47
Consolidation 102, 103
Conyngham Valley 63
Coughlin 85
Crestwood Industrial Park 17
Crestwood School District 103

D

Dairy farming 47
Dallas 15
Delawares 21, 23
Depression 79, 81, 82, 86, 89
Discrimination 60, 107
Diversity 12, 78
Dorrance 53, 55
Drumheller, Jacob 30
Durkee, Major John 24
Duryea 54

E

Earth Conservancy 107
Eastern Rite Catholicism 55
Economy 15, 92-94, 98, 102
Education 42, 52, 58, 88, 89, 91, 92, 99, 102, 104
Edwardsville 55, 56, 86, 102
Episcopalians 38
Ethnic heritage 16, 54, 78, 105, 106
Evangelical United Brethern 46
Exeter 26

F

Fairmount Springs 53
Fell, Judge Jesse 34
Flood Victims Action Council 98
Flood, Congressman Daniel J. 96
Flood of 1972 100
Football 79
Forty Fort 24-26, 97, 102
Freeland 18
Fugmann, Michael 76

G

G.A.R. 83
Garment industry 58, 94
Geography 12
Georgetown 55
Glen Lyon 52, 55
Gore, Obadiah and Daniel 33
Great Depression 81
Great Strike of 1902 62, 75
Greater Nanticoke Area School District 102

H

Hanover Area School District 103
Hanover Township 53, 54, 76, 103
Harvey's Lake 15, 19, 105
Hazleton 12, 14, 17-19, 30, 37, 39, 40, 42, 44, 45, 48, 52, 54-57, 60, 61, 63, 77, 82, 83, 85, 88, 89, 92-96, 99-101, 103, 104, 106-108
Hazleton Area School District 103
High school athletics 83
Historic Preservation District 16, 104
Hoban, Bishop Michael 59
Hodur, Bishop Francis 59
Hughestown 54
Hunlock Creek 82
Huntington Mills 80

I

Immigration 19, 51, 53, 59, 63, 78, 79, 86, 107
- Asian 106
- chain migration 57
- Croation 52
- English 42
- German 17, 45
- Greek 52
- Hispanics 107
- Hungarian 52
- Irish 43
- Italian 52
- Jewish 52, 55
- Lebanese 52
- Lithuanian 52
- Polish 52
- Ruthenian 52
- Scandinavian 52
- Serbian 52
- Slovak 52
- Slovenian 52
- statistics 51
- Syrian 52
- the immigrant experience 57
- Tyrolian 52
- Ukrainian 52
- Welsh 42
- Yankee 15

Industrial development 18, 52, 58, 63, 92-94
Iroquois 21, 22, 25, 28

J

Jeansville 40
Jeddo 13, 40
Jennings, Hughie 54

K

Kanjorski, Congressman Paul 107
King's College 8, 19, 88, 104
Kingston 19, 21, 25, 39, 42, 53, 55, 57, 83, 85, 97, 100, 102, 105
Knights of Labor 60
Knox Mine disaster 40, 77, 89
Ku Klux Klan 80

L

Labor unrest 75, 76
Lake Silkworth 53
Larksville 53, 102
Lattimer 40, 61
Lenni Lenape 21
Lewis, John L. 75
Lutherans 30
Luzerne 102
Luzerne County 6, 8, 11-16, 18, 19, 21, 22, 24, 26, 28-31, 33, 36-45, 47, 48, 51-63, 75, 76, 78-89, 91-93, 97-99, 101, 102, 104-108
- Court House 99
- founded 11
- statistics 13
- tour 19

Luzerne County Community College 104

M

Maconaqua 27, 53
Mahicans 21
Maloney, Thomas 76
Maronite Rite 56
Martin, Sheriff James 61
Masons 78, 80
Methodists 15, 30

Meyers High School 83
Mill Creek 23
Miners Mills 56
Mining 14, 40, 77, 92
Mitchell, John L. 61
Mohawks 22
Mohegans 21
Moravians 23
Mountaintop 14, 17, 19, 30, 47, 63, 82, 100, 101, 103

N

Nanticoke 15, 19, 21, 25, 36, 39, 40, 42, 52, 55-57, 59, 82-85, 97, 102, 104, 108
Native Americans 23, 27, 28, 36, 106
Nescopeck 18, 29
New Deal 86
Newport Township 29
North Mountain 18
North Branch Canal 35, 36, 43
Nottingham Colliery 40, 76

O

O'Hara, Bishop William 59
Oak Hill 82
Ogden, Captain Amos 23
Organized labor 60

P

Pardeesville 40
Patch towns 18
Patterson, Alexander 29
Paxtang Boys 25
Pennamites 24
Pennsylvania Dutch 17, 63
Pennsylvania State University 89, 104
Penobscot Mountain 17
Pentacostal Church 60
Pittston 15, 19, 21, 25, 35, 36, 39, 40, 42, 44, 53-57, 59, 63, 76, 77, 86, 89, 102, 108
Pittston Area School District 102
Pittston Hospital 89
Plains 21, 52, 103
Plymouth 21, 23, 25, 34, 39, 40, 42, 52, 54-57, 59, 76, 78, 82, 83, 85, 97, 100, 102
Poconos 14
Polish Alliance 78
Polish National Catholic Church 59
Population 13, 15-17, 22, 25, 28-30, 42, 46, 48, 51, 53, 55, 57, 63, 78-82, 85, 88, 89, 91, 100, 101, 103, 106
Poverty 60
Presbyterians 25, 38
Primitive Methodists 42
Pringle 86, 102
Protestants 43

R

Railroads 36, 60, 75
Reformed churches 30
Reformed Jews 46
Robinson, John 35
Roman Catholicism 44
Russian Orthodox Church 59

S

Seneca 26
Shawnee 21
Sisters of Mercy 80, 104
Sports 79
Pittston 54
Nanticoke 84
St. Stanislaus' Roman Catholic Church 52
Statistics 51, 77, 81, 96, 100
Stegmaier Brewery 46
Suburbanization 100
Sugarloaf 28
Sugar Notch 55
Sullivan's March 36
Susquehanna River 13-15, 19, 21-25, 31, 35-37, 40, 77, 96, 97
Susquehannah Company 22
Swoyersville 55, 56, 102

T

Temperature 14
Tilghman, James 33
Tinsley, Esther J. 89
Transportation 17, 36, 37, 51, 60, 75, 95
Tuscarora 21
Twin Shaft disaster 40

U

Unemployment 60, 96
Unionization 60
United Anthracite Miners of Pennsylvania 76
United Mine Workers 60, 61, 75

V

Valmont Industrial Park 96

W

Wanamie 55
Weiser, Conrad 23
Westmoreland 25, 28, 38
West Pittston 19, 102
White Haven 16
Wickeiser, Conrad 30
Wilkes-Barre Area School District 103
Wilkes-Barre/Scranton International Airport 37
Wilkes-Barre 13, 18, 19, 27, 31, 54, 55, 99, 104
Wilkes University 19, 88, 104
Women in the workforce 58
World War I 51, 62, 63, 75, 78
World War II 16, 17, 37, 54, 77, 79, 81-83, 85, 87-89, 92, 93, 104
Wyoming 35-40, 47, 53
Wyoming Area School District 102
Wyoming Valley 8, 12, 14-19, 21, 23-26, 29-31, 33, 35, 37-40, 42, 43, 60, 63, 76, 77, 83, 85, 92, 96, 97, 99-103, 107
Wyoming Valley West School District 85, 102

Y

Yankee-Pennamite Wars 25, 29

Z

Zinzendorf, Count von 23